Military History o

THE BATTLE
FOR KILMALLOCK

MILITARY HISTORY
OF THE IRISH CIVIL WAR

THE BATTLE
FOR KILMALLOCK

JOHN O'CALLAGHAN

SERIES EDITOR: GABRIEL DOHERTY

MERCIER PRESS

MERCIER PRESS

Cork

www.mercierpress.ie

© Text: John O'Callaghan, 2011

© Foreword: Gabriel Doherty, 2011

Reprinted 2022

ISBN: 978 1 85635 692 3

A CIP record for this title is available from the British Library

Printed and bound in the EU.

CONTENTS

ACKNOWLEDGEMENTS

I wish to thank Pádraig Óg Ó Ruairc for originally suggesting that I might wish to attempt to put order on the chaos that was the battle for Kilmallock. Pádraig was brave enough to read the first draft and the manuscript was a better one for his suggestions. Shane Walsh provided not only historical advice but tremendous technical skill in the production of the maps on pages 14 and 86, which add so much to the text. The map on page 107 is based on one originally produced by Eoin Neeson. Des Long generously shared his insights about the activities of both his father and father-in-law as IRA Volunteers in Limerick during the period of this study. Paul V. Walsh, Tom Toomey and David Costelloe shared their knowledge on the military history of the Civil War. Francis E. Maguire granted permission for the inclusion of excerpts from the diaries of John Pinkman, a participant in the battle for Kilmallock. Mike Maguire of Limerick City Library, Keith Murphy of the National Photographic Archive and Brian Hodkinson of Limerick City Museum offered invaluable assistance. Credit is also due to the staffs of the following archival institutions and libraries: the National Archives of Ireland and England; the National Library of Ireland; the Military Archives of Ireland; University College Dublin Archives; and the Imperial War Museum, London. At Mercier Press, it was a pleasure to work with Wendy Logue, who is a paragon of patience, and Mary

Feehan, who is a challenging editor. Any errors which remain are mine alone.

Do Mhairéad, Seán Óg agus Donncha – grá mo chroí sibh.

FOREWORD

At first glance Kilmallock, a small market town in the south of County Limerick, was an unlikely, almost unprepossessing, location for one of the largest and most protracted military engagements on the island of Ireland, not just of the Irish Civil War, but of Irish history generally in the modern era. Neither the town proper, nor its extended hinterland, offered any obvious or decisive prize to the contending parties. There were no significant strategic or economic targets in the vicinity (beyond the fact that the region generally was located in that particularly fertile zone known as the 'Golden Vale'); few significant communication channels such as canals or major rivers were in evidence, with the exception of the admittedly important railway line between Cork and Dublin, and a number of under-developed roads; and no sites of major symbolic importance were to be found nearby. Topographically, too, it was unremarkable, with the ranges of small hills (which were to play a significant role in the battle) that bordered the town the exception to the generally flat terrain of the environs. In short it was a rather mundane locale for events that were anything but mundane.

The causes, course and consequences of the battle are adroitly outlined in the following pages, and they make for a multifaceted amalgam of intent, luck, judgement (good and bad), planning, accident, parochialism, nationalism, honour and, in instances where evidence exists of the severe ill-treatment of prisoners of war, disgrace. In short, as in all such encounters, the full range of human virtues and vices was on display throughout.

One of the most praiseworthy aspects of John O'Callaghan's approach is his refusal to accept the 'inherited wisdom' regarding the engagement, and his determination to anchor the discussion as firmly as possible in the extant primary sources. This sound methodology enables him to rectify errors in the conventional account (some of which can be traced to the earliest professional studies of the Civil War), such as the very date of the battle itself. This historiographical fog of war is a formidable obstacle to a balanced understanding of the event, especially as it encompasses not just the differing perceptions and recollections of the two sides, but also their respective numerous subtle, and not-so-subtle, internal differences (which, inevitably, were more telling for the losing, Republican side).

What is clear, however, is that the battle marked a juncture in the war, between the open, mobile, conventional warfare of its decisive early weeks (albeit warfare waged by opposing forces ill-at-ease with the demands of same), and the drawn-out, excruciating, guerrilla phase. The estimate of around 1,600 participants in the fight seems reasonable, with the Free State army (as happened with surprising frequency during its advance to the south and west) finding itself at a serious numerical disadvantage during the final assault on Kilmallock itself. That they prevailed nonetheless can be attributed to several factors, not the least of which was the precipitate departure of many Cork and Kerry natives from the town's Republican garrison upon hearing word of the successful landings of pro-Treaty forces at several points along the south-west coastline. This co-ordination of a well-executed plan (Operation Order No. 6) at the local, tactical level with more ambitious strategic flanking movements, was but one illustration of the superior generalship on display on the Free State side during this first phase of the war – although the author quite correctly points out that some key decisions taken by the pro-Treaty commanders were by no means beyond reproach.

The concluding pages of the study are sobering indeed, for the author firmly rebuts the 'comforting myth' that the generally low casualty figures reflected a reluctance to kill fellow country-men and former comrades. On the contrary, all the evidence points to a growing mutual antipathy which could only widen and deepen the longer the conflict went on, and which inevitably manifested itself in ever-more vicious blows and counter-blows. It is a cautionary thought that the denizens of Kilmallock, for all that they were witness to significant bloodshed during the final days of July and the early days of August 1922, may have been the lucky ones, when their experiences are compared with the misery that was to be visited upon civilians in the zone of guerrilla operations a few miles to the south, which started just a few weeks later.

Gabriel Doherty
Department of History
University College Cork

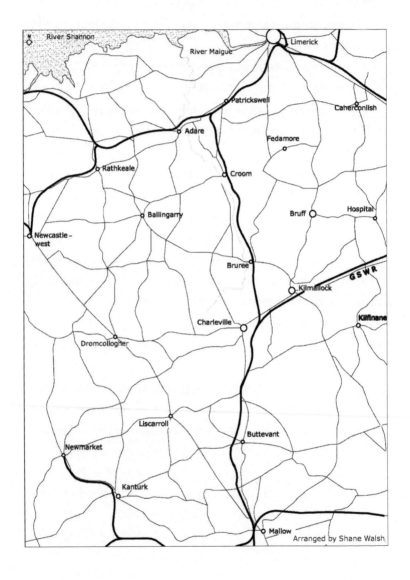

Introduction

The battle for Kilmallock was one of the largest engagements of the Irish Civil War and one of the most prolonged in duration. The objective of this book is to contextualise the military state of affairs and the political situation before the battle, and to outline the goals of the opposing forces and the stakes of victory and defeat at Kilmallock. It also seeks to assess the respective strengths of the forces involved in terms of their numbers, armaments, discipline and communications; to chart the course of the combat over more than two weeks; to consider the outcome of the fighting; and to evaluate its wider significance.

The War of Independence fought by the Irish Republican movement against British rule in Ireland resulted in a truce on 11 July 1921. The Anglo-Irish Treaty was signed in London on the morning of 6 December 1921, but proved divisive. Internal tensions, which had been buried or lain dormant during the previous 'four glorious years', soon resulted in a split in the Republican movement. The resulting Civil War has proven largely resistant to productive general overviews by historians, with only a few notable exceptions. Local studies concentrating on the causes, courses and consequences of the military aspects of the Civil War have, in some respects, been the most successful in revealing its intricate and often contradictory nature.

The body of historical scholarship on the Irish revolution, including the Easter Rising of 1916, the War of Independence and the Civil War, has matured appreciably in recent years. We now know and understand a great deal about the key dynamics in the revolutionary process but, conversely, there is still much that we do not know or understand. As the centenaries of the seminal transitions which constituted the revolutionary period of *c.* 1916–23 draw near, interest among academics and the public gathers unrelenting pace. What form and character potential new controversies may take – over the Civil War in particular – remains unclear, but debates and arguments can only be settled based on historical evidence. This book provides some of that evidence.

The language and phraseology employed by historians, particularly when dealing with a politically charged and emotionally resonant subject such as the Civil War, can carry significant symbolic meaning and involve important ideological implications. Contentious or problematic terminology should not be avoided simply to circumvent debate but, similarly, value-laden or pejorative terms should not be courted simply to provoke controversy. Contemporaneous terms can be rich, revealing and compelling, but they can carry with them underlying partisan implications, betraying a pro-Treaty or anti-Treaty agenda. They should be used sparingly and with caution. Treatyite propagandists, for instance, coined the term 'Irregular' to emphasise the legitimacy of the 'regular' pro-Treaty forces and the illegitimacy of the anti-Treaty forces. In this book, the pro-Treaty side will be variously referred to as the Free State, Provisional Government or National Army. The anti-Treaty side will be described as the Irish Republican Army (IRA) or Republicans, without necessarily endorsing the assumption that pro-Treatyites were not Republican.

KILMALLOCK

The battle for Kilmallock began after the fall of Limerick city to pro-Treaty forces on 21 July 1922 and culminated in the occupation of the town by the same forces on 5 August 1922 after anti-Treaty forces had evacuated. Developments in the interim were highly complex, erratic and often confusing. They do not lend themselves easily to a simple chronological approach. The fighting took place not in the town of Kilmallock itself, but was concentrated primarily in its immediate south Limerick hinterland of Bruff and Bruree.

Republicans chose this zone to make their next determined stand after Limerick city because it had considerable strategic importance. Kilmallock and the villages of Bruff and Bruree formed a rough triangle, with Bruff at the apex, about fifteen miles south of Limerick. Bruff is about six miles north-east of Kilmallock and Bruree is about four miles north-west. Kilmallock, in particular, as the first large town between Limerick city and the Cork border, was worth defending. The location of Charleville, a major town in north Cork, only a few miles south of both Bruree and Kilmallock, raised the stakes even further. Possession of Bruff and Bruree would be crucial in the battle for Kilmallock, since the IRA planned to use them as protective buffers. Patrickswell, about thirteen miles north of Bruree on the main road to the city, was also a factor because it straddled the primary route west from Limerick to Adare, Rathkeale, Newcastlewest, Abbeyfeale, and on to north Kerry.

The Bruff-Bruree-Kilmallock triangle presented a strong barrier to a Provisional Government advance from Limerick city on the heartland of the so-called Munster Republic, which was an almost exclusive bastion of anti-Treatyism. It lay south of a notional defensive line from Limerick city in the west, bordered on the north by the River Shannon, to Waterford city in the east, flanked by the River Suir. Republican commander Liam Deasy, Officer Commanding (O/C) 1st Southern Division IRA, explained that 'A defence line extending from Kilmallock to Bruree was established in the hope of holding the south.'[1] The Republican plan was to hold this area to stop the Free State army from advancing on Cork from their base in Limerick. Their position here would also act as a threat to the flank of any Free State advance westwards to the Kerry border.

Furthermore, Kilmallock controlled the intersection of a number of major roads, as well as being in close proximity to the main Dublin–Cork railway line and only fifteen miles from Limerick Junction. It was an ideal base from which to protect, or indeed sabotage, infrastructure.

The geography of Kilmallock also lent itself to a stubborn defence. Kilmallock Hill, Quarry Hill and Ash Hill each overlook Kilmallock, from the north, the north-east and the south-west respectively. They are little more than half a mile from the town itself, which sits in a depression on the banks of the River Loobagh. Knocksouna Hill, two miles to the west of Kilmallock, was also significant. The surrounding hills dominated the approaches to the town and, as such, were key to the control of Kilmallock. If the anti-Treaty forces in Kilmallock could maintain their hold on these heights, then wresting control of the town from them would be extremely problematic for the Free State army. Republicans who had retreated from Limerick city, together with local IRA units and anti-Treaty veterans from Cork and Kerry, maintained a significant presence in the Bruff-Bruree-Kilmallock triangle in south Limerick until early August. Anti-Treaty forces also briefly held Patrickswell at the start of the month. They were driven from all of these positions by 5 August, however, and were dislodged from Adare, Newcastlewest and Rathkeale in west Limerick by mid-August

THE POLITICAL BACKGROUND

There is no universally acceptable basis of identifiable fact and objective truth which can accommodate fundamentally competing interpretations, but any attempt to sum up the causes of the Civil War should consider the role of the Free State, the IRA and the British government. Joe Lee has made the essential point that the 'intimidatory gunman lurking in the shadows' of Irish politics under the Union was British.[2] The critical factor in the structure of Irish politics was the overwhelming superiority of British firepower: the threat made by the Prime Minister, David Lloyd George, of 'immediate and terrible war' hastened the conclusion of Anglo-Irish negotiations in London in December 1921.

The Treaty was in large part a British diktat, and the Irish plenipotentiaries were, arguably, cowed into submission (although some of them, including Michael Collins, might simply have felt they were getting the best deal available). Dáil Éireann began to debate the Treaty on 14 December 1921 and endorsed it by a small majority (by 64 to 57) on 7 January 1922.

The arguments raised for and against recognition of the Treaty were, for the most part, reasonably uncomplicated. The issue of partition was not prominent because most shades of Republican opinion simply assumed that the measure was temporary – to placate Unionists – and that the situation would right itself in due course.

Éamon de Valera was one of the minority in cabinet – three of seven – who opposed the Treaty. His main arguments were that the character of the Treaty was incompatible with the Republican nature of the Dáil, that the delegates had exceeded their authority and that, consequently, even if a majority of Dáil deputies voted in favour of the Treaty, he and his supporters would not feel duty-bound to abide by their decision.

The Treaty had the prerequisite that TDs would be obliged to take an oath of allegiance to the British Crown. This proved particularly objectionable to many Republicans and their concern was mirrored by the fixation of British monarchists with attaining symbolic supremacy. The British had seemingly been prepared to return to war on this point and the oath was also one of the main reasons why the anti-Treaty Irish Republicans were later willing to engage in civil war.

Those in favour of the Treaty argued that it granted Ireland a degree of freedom which could be used as a stepping-stone towards complete independence. Collins stressed that it was not the signing of the Treaty which represented the fatal compromise on the status of the Republic, but the initial agreement to negotiate. Likewise, the binding nature of the Treaty was bestowed on it not by its original signing in London, but by its ratification in the Dáil.

The press and the Catholic Church employed their substantial resources and influence in support of the Treaty. For instance, anti-Treatyite Liam Manahan of Ballylanders, an East Limerick IRA Brigade veteran,[3] asserted that his local Dáil member for Limerick City–Limerick East, Colonel Liam Hayes from Kilteely, had opposed the Treaty until the parish priest convinced him otherwise.[4] The fact that the debate extended over the Dáil Christmas break, however, was perhaps even more important. The encounter that TDs had with local public opinion at this stage certainly influenced some towards ratification of the Treaty when they might otherwise have voted against it. Limerick County Council called on the Dáil to do everything possible to arrive at a unanimous decision on the issue.[5]

In fact, Dáil unanimity was not essential. Disagreement *without disruption* would not have led to civil war. It did not matter what the Dáil and the politicians did, so much as what the IRA and the military men did. Thus, it was not the split among the political leaders of the Dáil that caused the Civil War – it was the rift within the IRA. It is reasonable to assume that even had the Dáil been unanimous in ratifying the Treaty there would have been some resistance to civil authority by sections of the IRA. Previous attempts by the Dáil during the War of Independence to bring the army fully under its control had not been completely successful. There was no tradition of political control of militant Republicanism, and ultimately, the IRA was beholden to itself alone.

There has been something of a trend among historians towards extolling the constitutional and democratic virtues of the pro-Treaty position while simultaneously deprecating the anti-Treaty position as anti-democratic, authoritarian and dictatorial. The reality is that most pro- and anti-Treatyites took sides before they knew which way the Dáil vote or any subsequent election would go. Many members of the IRA appear to have decided their stance on the Treaty quite independently of the national leadership.

The split within the IRA was caused by many local, non-political factors, of which local leadership seems to have been the most important. The nature of the guerrilla campaign of 1919–21 had necessitated a parochial structure in which local IRA Volunteers knew and trusted each other. The level of control exercised by IRA General Headquarters (GHQ) in Dublin over units around the country was often very limited and this had ramifications when the movement splintered in the run-up to the Civil War.

The war developed along political as well as military lines, however. De Valera did not cause the war but, in his efforts to claw his way back from the sidelines and reclaim his leadership role, he did not do as much as he might have to prevent it. He also did much that was harmful (though some of his militarist rhetoric may have been misreported at the time). The conduct of the war was outside his influence, although he was certainly able to manipulate the Treaty in the late 1920s and 1930s, shaping it to his own political purposes and deriving benefit from it for the country at large. His pursuit of radical support from the army further destabilised the situation, even though the army paid little enough attention to him in the run-up to the war.

De Valera resigned as president of the Dáil and was replaced by Arthur Griffith. De Valera and the other anti-Treaty TDs withdrew from the Dáil, taking with them any hopes for a smooth and orderly implementation of the terms of the Treaty. On 14 January 1922 the one and only meeting of the parliament of southern Ireland, as established under the 1920 Government of Ireland Act, set up the 'Provisional Government' under the chairmanship of Michael Collins. Thus, there was a dual system of power in place, though membership of the Dáil cabinet and the Provisional Government largely overlapped.

Some of the terms of the Treaty were implemented in an effort to illustrate the independence which the country enjoyed after official control over the political administration of the twenty-six counties was transferred to the Provisional Government on 16 January 1922:

- The Irish Free State was scheduled to come into being on 6 December 1922.
- A committee empowered to draft the constitution of the new state came together.
- British forces began to evacuate the country.
- Procedures for a general election were set in train.
- Initial moves were made to create a new police force (an Garda Síochána) to replace the discredited and demoralised Royal Irish Constabulary.
- Initial moves were also made to establish an Irish army from pro-Treaty units of the IRA.

There were several, varied pro-Treaty perspectives. Collins and

Griffith, for instance, may well have supported the Treaty for very different reasons. Collins probably regarded it as a tactical delaying manoeuvre. Griffith, although never as comfortable as Collins with the physical force element of the Republican campaign for independence, was fully committed to the Treaty and had little doubt that its terms were the best that Ireland could realistically have hoped to achieve. Griffith was intolerant of opposition to the Treaty and was determined to crush all dissent quickly, even if it meant civil war, but he was initially restrained by Collins. Most elements of the anti-Treaty side were reluctant to commit to a military campaign until the Free State constitution was published.

The electoral pact agreed between Collins and de Valera on 20 May 1922 aimed to preserve the fragile strands of unity which remained between the pro- and anti-Treaty sides. Approved by the Dáil and the Sinn Féin party, it seemed to hold out the possibility of a peaceful solution. It was contingent on a constitution with a Republican character and an electoral procedure (albeit a somewhat undemocratic one that prevented voters from directly expressing their opinion on the Treaty), which would guarantee coalition government and shared cabinet participation.

The immovable obstacle to its implementation was the objection of the British government. The pact fell apart in the days before the election and the proposed constitution of the Free State was redrafted to satisfy Lloyd George. The chief architect of the amended final document was legal expert Hugh Kennedy, working under Griffith's supervision and in consultation with the British representative Lord Hewart. It was published on the morning of general election day, 16 June. Of 620,283 ballots, pro-Treaty Sinn Féiners won 239,193 and anti-Treaty Sinn Féiners 133,864, while other candidates secured 247,226 votes. This amounted to a large pro-Treaty majority. Significantly, 40 per cent of the electorate supported non-Sinn Féiners. Fifty-eight pro-Treaty candidates were returned, thirty-six anti-Treaty, seventeen Labour, seven Farmers' Party, six Independents and four Dublin University representatives.

Most of those elected in the two Limerick constituencies had impeccable Republican and revolutionary credentials before the split on the Treaty. The pro-Treaty TDs for Limerick City–Limerick East were Richard Hayes, a veteran of the 1916 Rising, and Liam Hayes, who had taken part in the Dromkeen ambush of 1921. The anti-Treaty TDs were Michael Colivet, commandant of the Limerick City Volunteers in 1916, and Kathleen O'Callaghan, whose husband Michael (a former lord mayor of Limerick) was assassinated by Crown forces in 1921. The pro-Treaty TDs for Kerry–Limerick West were Piaras Béaslaí, a member of the Irish Republican Brotherhood; James Crowley, another War of Independence veteran; and Fionán Lynch of the National Army. The anti-Treaty TDs were Patrick Cahill of the 1st Kerry Brigade; the Fenian Con Collins from Newcastlewest; Austin Stack, who had been sentenced to death (but reprieved) after the 1916 Rising; and Thomas O'Donoghue and Edmund Roche, both of whom had first been elected in 1921.

Brian Murphy, in charting the evolution of anti-Treaty perspectives in the six months between its signing and the outbreak of the Civil War, contends that opposition to the Treaty alone was the initial impetus, but that attitudes hardened when the determining influence of the British government in the implementation of the Treaty became apparent:

> The British government was the final arbiter of the Free State Constitution; it was the British government that insisted the Pact approved by Dáil Éireann had to be broken; it was the British government that had insisted on an election for an Ireland of twenty-six counties rather than for an all Ireland Dáil Éireann. Moreover, it was the British government that was supplying arms to the Free State Army; and it was the British government that had ordered those arms to be used against the IRA in the Four Courts [occupied in April 1922 by an anti-Treaty faction under Rory O'Connor in clear defiance of the Provisional Government]. Republicans argued that, in such circumstances, it was not only reasonable, but also necessary to fight for a Republic.[6]

On 19 August 1922, a letter from Ernie O'Malley commenting on the Republican position in light of the recent general election result appeared in the *Irish Independent* under the heading 'What Republicans Fight For'. 'Know then that this is true', he wrote:

1. The Republicans who are engaged in this war are fighting in a just and holy cause – namely, the defence of the Republic to which they have sworn to be faithful.

2. The attack on them has no authority from the Irish people.

At the recent elections the people voted for the pact and peace, for Labour and peace, for the farmers and peace, for the Independents and peace. No one voted for war.

3. The Dáil was not consulted before this war was launched. It was undertaken at the bidding of England before the Dáil met.

4. The people who accepted the Treaty did so because they thought it would give peace. The alternative [that] had been put before them was possibly war with England. If the other alternative had been put before them, namely that the Treaty meant certain war between ourselves, they would never have considered the Treaty.

Desmond FitzGerald's (unpublished) reply addressed and countered each of O'Malley's points:

(1) The Republicans are engaged in a 'just and holy' war in 'defence of the Republic'. This is a mis-statement. The Parliament of the Republic ratified a Treaty with Great Britain, and the Irregulars have gone into insurrection against its authority.

(2) 'At the recent elections the people voted for the pact and peace.' This is false. The people voted not for the pact but for the Treaty, as proved beyond doubt by the fact that in every case the anti-Treaty members lost their seats to Independent candidates.

(3) 'The Dáil was not consulted before this war was launched.' Quite true. The Irregular leaders did not consult An Dáil when they seized Irish public buildings, looted Irish property, kidnapped an Irish general, and notified England that the Truce made with her by the Dáil was at an end.

(4) 'The people who accepted the Treaty did so because they thought it would give peace.' This statement is utterly inconsistent with point (2). But is true, and merely serves to demonstrate the wickedness of the Irregulars' action. They admit that the people wanted peace, and they therefore give them war.[7]

Republicans did not think of their actions as anti-democratic because they believed that the Republic, which they had sworn to uphold, could not legitimately be disestablished. The electoral majority of 1922 did not count in their eyes because of the threat of British coercion. The Republic rested on the moral sacrifice of 1916 and the popular mandate of the 1918 all-island general election. More technically minded Republicans referred to the failure to dissolve the second Dáil in 1922. The purpose here, however, is not to validate or repudiate the respective pro- and anti-Treaty positions, but to clarify what motivated people at the time and to explain the strengths and limitations of a particular argument, whether in terms of its logic or its potential to generate support. The results of the general election, skewed as it was in many ways by the threat of war, provide some basis on which to proceed.

Plenipotentiaries had signed the Treaty. A cabinet majority

subsequently accepted it. It was also endorsed by a majority of Dáil Éireann, and it had won the backing of a substantial majority of the Irish electorate. This played a significant role in establishing the status and credibility of the Free State government and undermining the anti-Treaty case. The ability of the Free State to get a functioning administration in place was vital, giving it authority and power. It provided a concrete rallying point for civilian supporters. The church and press had bestowed explicit moral licence on the Treaty and the Free State, while denying it to the anti-Treatyites and effectively casting them in the role of heretics.

NON-COMBATANTS: CIVILIANS, THE PRESS AND 'HEARTS AND MINDS'

The general election vote also demonstrated a widespread desire for stability and action on pressing social and economic issues, as well as a growing apathy to ideological abstractions. Both sides therefore displayed a keen awareness of the importance of courting civilian support, or at least of not alienating the civilian population, with the positive result that it was rarely targeted by either side.

Among the Republican units in the Kilmallock area in July and August 1922 were H Company from Kiskeam in Duhallow, North Cork (No. 2) Brigade. One of them noted how:

> ... the farmers and milking teams would go about their milking morning and evening despite the skirmishing between the

warring parties and the fact that bullets were whistling over-head and around the fields as they milked. At first the local people were fearful, but gradually they ignored the fighting and went about their work.[8]

Agricultural work, like many other forms of labour, was severely disrupted at the time, however, and livestock often fell victim to stray bullets and perhaps occasionally to deliberately aimed bullets. Anecdotal evidence suggests that a farmer in Adare lost a bull during the fighting when an IRA Lewis gunner from Limerick city was startled by the animal and resorted to his weapon for protection, cutting the beast in two.

A distinct advantage which the National Army enjoyed over the IRA when it came to dealing with civilians was the fact that they were paid by the Provisional Government and could thus purchase supplies. The IRA often had only limited supplies of food and money and no means of obtaining credit. The issue of commandeering and forced levies often caused friction between Republicans and local civilians, and there was often at least some truth in the claim, which regularly appeared in newspaper accounts of the arrival of Free State forces in areas where Republicans had previously held sway, that there was great joy at the relief of the town, with the people coming out to welcome the troops. On Wednesday 27 July 1922, for instance, *Sgéal Chatha Luimnighe (Limerick War News)* included an article headlined 'The Robbers':

A gang of irregulars made a descent on the village of Rathkeale on Monday evg., and looted several shops. They have seized thousands of pounds worth of goods in this town since they commenced their attempt to subvert the National Government. No wonder the people have come to refer to them as 'the robbers'.

The great drawback of such a concentration of Republican troops as there was in south Limerick was that of supplies. Food and shelter were most readily available to the anti-Treatyites in the towns, which explains why most of the early battles of the war were fought in and around larger population centres. The National Army was thus facilitated in bringing to bear its advantage in heavy equipment, particularly artillery. The IRA had no artillery and no anti-artillery defences. Their expertise lay in conducting brief ambushes rather than staging conventional battles. The level of civilian support which had allowed Republicans to compensate for their deficiencies in transport, supplies and communications during the guerrilla campaign of the War of Independence was no longer forthcoming.

One of the main arenas in which the battle for hearts and minds was fought was newspaper censorship and suppression. *Sgéal Chatha Luimnighe* was produced by the forces of the Free State in Limerick city from mid-July to mid-August. It was the mouthpiece of the pro-Treaty side and carried official bulletins on the progress of the war in Limerick city and county and around the country. These bulletins were issued from the publicity department, field GHQ, South Western Command, which was based in Cruise's Hotel in the city. The *Limerick Leader* did not appear between 30 June and 13 October. Editions of the *Limerick Chronicle* were published on 8 July and again on 22 July (headed 11–22 July). This absence is easily accounted for by the battle for Limerick city. The *Chronicle* appeared regularly then until 12 August but after this not again until 17 October. The 12 August edition explained the political background and the economic rationale behind the decision to temporarily suspend publication:

> Early in July an intimation was conveyed to each office from the irregular forces that 'all war news dealing with the present situation' must be submitted for censorship at the New barracks before publication. As it was considered undesirable to submit to this censorship it was decided that the four [local newspaper] offices be closed down, and no local newspaper appeared for a fortnight. On July 22nd, in order to give reliable information to the public, much harm having been done by the circulation of false rumours, publication was resumed, but under conditions which rendered a heavy loss on every issue inevitable. Owing to the complete stagnation of trade most of our advertisers have cancelled their orders, so that the receipts from advertisements have been practically nil. Except to a very limited extent within the past few days it has not been possible to send any papers either to agents or subscribers in the country; consequently only city sales could be counted on. For all these reasons it has been deemed necessary to suspend publication for the present, and we do so with the utmost regret, not wishing, if at all possible, to increase unemployment in the city.

Much of the material reported in the *Chronicle* overlapped with that in *Sgéal Chatha Luimnighe*. Republicans had no real local equivalent and were heavily defeated in the propaganda stakes in Limerick.

The battle for Kilmallock featured not only in the local and national press, but also in the international press. For instance, on 30 July 1922 *The New York Times* reported that 'all eyes are directed towards Kilmallock, where the fighting has been stubborn and the casualties numerous'. The information in *The New York Times* was often even more unreliable than that in the local papers, however.

THE MILITARY BACKGROUND

The backbone of the new Free State army was provided by the Dublin Guard, which came into being during the later stages of the War of Independence when the Active Service Unit of the Dublin Brigade and Michael Collins' assassination 'Squad' were amalgamated. This merger was necessary because of the heavy losses suffered by the Dublin Brigade in May 1921. Paddy Daly, formerly head of the Squad, took charge of the new elite unit, which took over Beggars Bush Barracks from the British army at the beginning of February 1922. The Dublin Guard supported the Treaty out of loyalty to Collins:

> Our leader was Mick Collins, idol of the nation, and for those of us in the Dublin Guards, at least, there was no other man in Ireland for whom we'd more gladly die.[9]

The Dublin Guard were among the most experienced and

committed of the National Army's troops, but like most of the sections in the new army, even they were not immune from occasional mutinies. Nonetheless, on the outbreak of the Civil War in June 1922 they were to the forefront in securing Dublin for the Free State. They also formed the spearhead of the Free State drive into the anti-Treaty stronghold of Munster in July and August, which included the battles for Limerick city and Kilmallock.

Private John Pinkman, a member of the Dublin Guard, recalled:

> The Dublin Guards Brigade had already established its reputation as the shock troops of the National Army – a sort of legion of the vanguard, one might say – and when we were chosen to spearhead the drive against the Kilmallock redoubt, we were proud of the honour.[10]

The advance units of the Dublin Guard were essentially mobile task formations. In terms of their military deployment, the practice of assembling small, motorised detachments and providing them with armoured vehicles and artillery became standard practice early in the war. National Army armoured vehicles and artillery served a number of purposes, not least as an effective and vital means of bolstering the morale and confidence of raw and inexperienced recruits.

Following an IRA convention in March 1922 (which Free State Minister for Defence Richard Mulcahy was unable to prevent), an executive was appointed which subsequently refused to recognise the authority of any civilian body. Supporters of the IRA Executive, led by Rory O'Connor, occupied the Four Courts in April.

Even after the June election, however, the majority of anti-Treaty military leaders did not wish to renew hostilities with the British forces, and certainly did not want to become embroiled in civil war. While twelve of sixteen members of the Military Council Executive voted to re-engage the Crown forces, the Army Convention rejected their proposal by 118 votes to 103, with Chief of Staff Liam Lynch being among the majority.[11] There had been an increasing number of violent incidents across the country since early in the year, however. This was indicative of the growing tension.

Open conflict between pro- and anti-Treaty forces in Limerick was only narrowly averted in the spring. On 18 February Brigadier Liam Forde of Mid Limerick repudiated the authority of GHQ and denounced the Treaty. Competition for control of strong points in the city after the British evacuation evolved into a crisis which very nearly precipitated civil war in the weeks after Forde's proclamation of loyalty to the Republic. Hostilities almost broke out as hundreds of fighters from outside were drafted into the city in a contest over which side would occupy the barracks there. Arthur Griffith urged an aggressive response to the challenge to governmental authority but Mulcahy refused to sanction an attack on the basis that the army was not yet up to the test. The resultant negotiated settlement prevented fighting in the short term.

At the start of July in Limerick city 700 Republicans under Liam Lynch, Liam Deasy and Seán Moylan, O/C North Cork

(No. 2) Brigade, faced 400 Provisional Government troops, drawn from the 1st Western and 4th Southern Divisions of the National Army under Michael Brennan and Donnchadh O'Hannigan respectively. Lynch and O'Hannigan came from the same parish, Anglesboro/Kilbehenny, in south-east Limerick. Lynch may have hoped that, along with his old colleagues Brennan and O'Hannigan, he could present a unified southern front to the Provisional Government and prevent the spread of the war from Dublin. The only possible way that civil conflict could have been restricted to Dublin, however, was if Lynch had marched the full array of forces under his command on the capital in a *coup d'état*. The defence of the Munster Republic seems to have been the only plan that the anti-Treatyite military leadership considered. This stance was simply too negative to hold out much real chance of success.

Lynch, in a huge tactical miscalculation, agreed a series of peace deals in Limerick city, which held until 11 July. This delay in fighting had been to the distinct advantage of pro-Treaty forces, who by July were no longer outnumbered and outgunned. Blissfully ignorant of these developments, and seemingly happy with the situation, Lynch moved his HQ from Limerick to Clonmel.

Sufficient additional troops, backed up by armoured cars, had been deployed to Limerick by that stage to allow Brennan to terminate the truce with confidence. Most of the fighting during the next ten days was localised around the Republican-occupied barracks. Government forces were continually being reinforced, but the fighting was indecisive until a field gun arrived from Dublin. Government forces began shelling anti-

Treaty fortified positions on 19 July. This allowed them to blast breaches in the Republican-held barracks. The Strand Barracks fell first, but only after a brave defence. By the end of 21 July, the Castle, Ordnance and New Barracks had all been evacuated and sabotaged. Many members of these garrisons retreated south.

As with overall casualty figures for the Civil War, complete accuracy is difficult to attain in respect of the fatalities incurred during the battle for Limerick city. *Sgéal Chatha Luimnighe* acknowledged as much on 25 July when it stated that 'The casualty list is heavs [*sic*], and the total of dead and wounded cannot be accurately estimated at present.' Nonetheless, this did not stop the paper from making a very confident, if inaccurate, estimation: 'It is definitely known however that 15 are dead, and 87 wounded, while it is generally believed that about 30 irregulars lost their lives.' The most reliable and authoritative figures available are those compiled by Pádraig Óg Ó Ruairc, which indicate that the fighting claimed the lives of twenty-two people – five Republicans, six pro-Treaty troops and eleven civilians.[12]

Both pro- and anti-Treaty protagonists retrospectively acknowledged that control of Limerick city was fundamental to the outcome of the war. From a Free State perspective, the pivotal strategic importance of the city was based on preventing the two critical pro-Treaty commands outside of Dublin – General Michael Brennan's in Clare and General Seán MacEoin's in Athlone – becoming isolated from each other. Brennan maintained that 'the whole Civil War really turned on Limerick'.[13] The Shannon river was a protective barrier as well as a means of access between the south and west. Brennan's forces in Clare separated the Munster Republic from other strong anti-Treaty areas to the north, on the west coast. The capture of Limerick by the Provisional Government served to reinforce the disconnect between Munster Republicans and those in Galway, Connemara, Mayo and parts of Sligo. It also meant that only the Bruff-Bruree-Kilmallock triangle prevented the National Army marching into Cork and Kerry.

THE COMMAND STRUCTURES

Liam Deasy and Seán Moylan were the principal Republican commanders during the battle for Kilmallock. Moylan happened to be a native of Kilmallock: he had joined the local Irish Volunteer Company in 1914 before he moved to Cork and rose through the ranks. The principal Free State commander was General Eoin O'Duffy, whose South Western Command included north Kerry, north Cork, Limerick and Clare, and parts of south Galway and north Tipperary. Like his Republican counterparts Deasy and Moylan, O'Duffy had been a senior IRA officer and was a veteran of guerrilla warfare. He had also been elected to Dáil Éireann in 1921.

O'Duffy's second-in-command was an even more experienced military campaigner. Major General William Richard English (W. R. E.) Murphy had joined the British army in 1914 as an officer cadet. He was in action from 1915 with the 1st Battalion of the South Staffordshire Regiment in France, Belgium and Italy, was promoted to the rank of lieutenant colonel and was awarded the Distinguished Service Order and the Military Cross. He left the army after the Great War and returned to Ireland in 1919.

Before the war Murphy had spent time at St Patrick's teacher training college in Dublin, where he met Gearóid O'Sullivan. In 1922 O'Sullivan, by then a general, called on his expertise during the organisation of the Free State army.[14] Michael Collins gave Murphy a commission on the strength of his military record, and with the outbreak of the Civil War he was appointed to a series of commands in the Free State army, serving in Kildare, Wicklow, Limerick, Kerry and Dublin. He was second in overall command of the National Army from January to May 1923, though his role in the battle for Limerick city is somewhat unclear. Pádraig Óg Ó Ruairc places him in the old William Street RIC barracks in the city before and during the battle.[15] Karl Murphy, however, suggests that he only arrived in Limerick after its evacuation by the IRA and that he had been appointed to the South Western Command on the basis of his performances at Blessington in Wicklow and Ballymore Eustace in Kildare in the middle of July, when he had impressed in his management of raw troops and his logistical competence.[16]

The partnership of O'Duffy with Murphy as his adjutant provided an ideal combination of IRA and conventional military force command experience. O'Duffy arrived in Limerick on Monday 17 July to assume personal command of pro-Treaty operations there. Once he had ousted the Republicans from their strongholds and taken the city, O'Duffy turned his attention to the rest of the county. He set about having plans drawn up for an advance by various National Army units to the south and west designed to drive the IRA out of Limerick.[17] This would allow for a land invasion of the Munster Republic, which would be executed in parallel with a series of coastal landings in Cork and Kerry. O'Duffy ordered Brigadier Michael Keane of Feohanagh to move south-west against the Republicans in Rathkeale, Askeaton, Foynes and Newcastlewest, before proceeding to Kerry.

The coastal landings were the idea of General Emmet Dalton, another veteran of the Great War. He presented them as an accompaniment to what would otherwise have been a more laborious and attritional overland campaign through towns and countryside and over mountainous, guerrilla-friendly territory. Avoiding this type of fighting as far as possible would save time, money and lives. The landings were also designed to draw the Cork and Kerry contingents away from Kilmallock.

Michael Collins and Richard Mulcahy, mindful of the problems encountered between Limerick city and Kilmallock, supported Dalton's proposal and both of its objectives were achieved.[18] When the landings took place, they proved to be hugely decisive in the context of Kilmallock because they became the primary concern of many of the Cork and Kerry Republicans there, some of whom abandoned their defensive positions in favour of attempting to repulse the invasion of their home territories. Michael Brennan's 1st Western Division returned to Clare from Limerick city to consolidate Provisional Government authority there. The Civil War was particularly bitter in Brennan's territory. Brennan had been O/C East Clare Brigade during the War of Independence. East Clare and Mid Clare had been fierce rivals, as was occasionally the case with neighbouring units which might be competing for supplies or glory. Personality clashes between individual commanders could also be a factor. The Free State executed five Mid Clare IRA anti-Treaty fighters during the Civil War, two of them in Limerick city and three of them in Brennan's divisional area.

THE SHAPE OF THE CIVIL WAR

On 22 June 1922 General Sir Henry Wilson was assassinated. His killing was most probably ordered by Collins in retaliation for Wilson's role in the spiralling sectarian violence in Northern Ireland, where he was security advisor to the government. The British, however, believed that Rory O'Connor's men in the Four Courts were responsible for Wilson's death. When the Republican garrison there took Free State Deputy Chief of Staff J. J. O'Connell prisoner on 27 June, it provided Collins with an opportunity to act against them without appearing to be simply doing Lloyd George's bidding. The Civil War officially started on 28 June when, at the instigation of Lloyd George, the Provisional Government shelled O'Connor's anti-Treaty faction in the Four Courts using British army field guns.

The anti-Treaty IRA was concentrated in Munster, which had earlier been the centre of anti-British activity. Leinster, which had been largely dormant in the War of Independence, was predominantly pro-Treaty, although the Dublin Brigade chose the anti-Treaty side. Connacht was divided in half: Mayo and Sligo were Republican; Roscommon, Leitrim and Galway were pro-Treaty. In general, those brigades which had been most active in the War of Independence went Republican and those which had been largely quiescent went pro-Treaty. There were exceptions of course: South Wexford, Sligo, Mayo and Kerry had participated little in the War of Independence, but were now anti-Treaty. Also, East Clare, East Limerick and North Tipperary, which had been among the most effective guerrilla units in 1919–21, went pro-Treaty.

IRA violence during 1919–21 was often designed to provoke reprisals, outrage public opinion and apply political pressure on the British government. The vast disparity in strength between the IRA and Crown forces meant that very little was directly decided by force of arms. Militarily, the early engagements of the Civil War were on a much greater scale than those of the War of Independence. Between late June and August 1922 the Provisional Government of the Irish Free State and the anti-Treaty IRA engaged each other in fairly evenly matched armed combat, on a much more conventional basis than during the earlier war between the guerrilla units of the IRA and Crown forces. This was not symbolic violence, designed to inspire myth or legend. The exclusive aim was to claim territory. The Civil War was a low-intensity conflict generally, and apart from during the early stages, fighting on any significant scale was intermittent.

Casualty rates are difficult to determine with any precision. Pádraig Óg Ó Ruairc estimates that there were about 1,500 deaths because of the war: 730 National Army troops, 350 anti-Treaty IRA members, and 400 civilians.[19] Michael Hopkinson was, with good cause, reluctant to cite an exact number. He did, however, suggest that Republican deaths would have been much more numerous than Free State deaths but that the figures of 4,000 or more total casualties cited by some sources were most likely exaggerated.[20] A useful comparison can be made with Finland in 1918, another small state which had recently acquired independence. It seems reasonable to suggest that total Irish fatalities in the war probably amounted to no more than 10 per cent of the 30,000 fatalities suffered in the Finnish Civil War of January to May 1918. While the war there was fought over a shorter time frame than in Ireland, it did involve significant German and Russian intervention. The Irish Civil War was far less ferocious.

While the War of Independence was not won or lost by fighting alone, direct military confrontation was clearly a much more critical factor in deciding the outcome of the Civil War. It was not, however, the decisive factor. The eventual victory of the pro-Treaty side in the Civil War came about in May 1923, almost eleven months after the initial government attack on the rebel-held Four Courts, principally because of the gradual dissolution of anti-Treaty Republican resistance rather than because of any spectacular battleground successes for the Free State. The death in action of Liam Lynch on 10 April 1923 and his replacement as Chief of Staff by Frank Aiken, who was perhaps more realistic in his assessment of the capability of his forces to continue the struggle, prompted a ceasefire on 30 April and the dumping of arms from 24 May.

The shortcomings of Republican political policy and military strategy and tactics were often matched by the incompetence of their pro-Treaty rivals and the outcome of the war was by no means a foregone conclusion. It is important to view what happened in the light of what could possibly have come to pass, and, in this sense, the war was initially a much more finely balanced affair than its denouement might suggest. John Pinkman was one of those who were dismissive of the anti-Treaty IRA as a fighting force:

> ... apart from the leadership of a few splendid fighters, such as Liam Lynch himself, who'd proved themselves during the Tan War against the British, the Irregular forces were only the shambles of an army. We had the insuperable advantage of being the National Army. We looked it ... and we proved it.[21]

The balance of manpower, weaponry and fighting experience, however, seemed initially to favour the Republicans but, vitally, the Free State held control of more of the important military installations around the country. Mobility was one of the fundamental features of the conventional phase of the Irish Civil War – the Free State had the greater resources, and consequently the advantage, in this regard as both sides needed to quickly establish their physical control over the country. The pro-Treaty forces dedicated themselves to this task with more gusto than their anti-Treaty rivals and won the race for territory. Eoin Neeson made the point that when the war began the pro-Treatyites held the key positions for moving against anti-Treaty strongholds: Nenagh against Limerick, Athlone against the midlands and north-west, and Kilkenny against the south-east.[22] By mid-July, with the exception of parts of the west and the Munster Republic, all the principal military posts in the country were in the hands of the pro-Treaty forces.

Given these circumstances, the reluctance of the Provisional Government to face down the anti-Treaty IRA reflected a lack of confidence in the new National Army. The stand-off in Limerick city in February and March exemplified this. There was not much more reason to be confident in the Provisional Government army by June. During the fighting in Dublin, the British military and political authorities repeatedly voiced their discomfort about the capacity of the army.[23] The Republicans had failed to capitalise on glaring pro-Treaty weaknesses before the commencement of hostilities, however, and these limitations, which were still readily apparent in the first weeks of the war, were gradually compensated for by the recruitment of an army of 30,000 men and a steady supply of British guns.

The Republican failure to forestall the government offensive and the muted response to it allowed the National Army to dictate the pace and direction of the war between the shelling of the Four Courts at the end of June and the shelling of Republican bases in Limerick city on 19 July. The reactionary and overly defensive stance assumed by the anti-Treatyites in the first months of the war gave the Free State the time it so badly needed. John Regan has argued, quite convincingly, that the Free State used this time to form a type of Treatyite military dictatorship, which was in place even before the death of Michael Collins on 22 August, as the army garnered control of civil functions and extra-constitutional powers within the regime.[24] The Republican concentration on holding the Munster Republic, combined with the contradictory abandonment of inland urban centres such as Kilmallock while the National Army was landing along the coast, proved a confused failure.

Michael Hopkinson likened Liam Lynch to the Grand Old Duke of York, moving his troops from point to point in futile scrambling manoeuvres.[25]

MILITARY CHARACTERISTICS OF THE BATTLE FOR KILMALLOCK

A remarkable characteristic of the Irish Civil War in terms of the history of the conduct of warfare is how dissimilar it was in operational procedure to the Great War of 1914–18. In Ireland there was nothing like the trench stalemate that dominated much of the war on the Western Front: the minor emphasis placed on trenches by W. R. E. Murphy during the battle for Kilmallock should not be exaggerated. This was because of the relatively small number of troops engaged, the even smaller number of heavy arms employed, and the policy of flight rather than fight often adopted by the Republican forces.

The efforts of the Free State to break the Republican grip on the Bruff-Bruree-Kilmallock triangle produced what might be called the only line battle or line fighting of the Civil War, with the opposing sides facing each other in a type of cross-country warfare with a fairly well-defined front line. Each side maintained a string of outposts in the triangle, at crossroads and on commanding hilltops, with a 'No-Man's Land' varying in width between 100 yards and a mile. John Pinkman recalled that Commandant Tom Flood established his headquarters in a farmhouse half a mile to the rear of the front line: 'I remember how we were glad of the big breakfasts and mugs of hot tea which we got in the farmhouse having lain out all night in the damp grass.'[26]

A journalist described the scene he witnessed in the area at the end of July:

> .. both sides are very chary about allowing anybody – man or woman, boy or girl – to pass through their lines, which, of course, is quite understandable. Sometimes it happens that outposts approach … and retire again without firing a shot, but as a rule there are sharp engagements when such close quarters are reached. A National officer on outpost duty told me that often he has crept so close to an irregular guard that he could hear them talking.[27]

This situation, unique in recent Irish military history, produced some of the war's most intense fighting, in which conventional engagements, focused around at least one set of the combatants attempting to hold or to take a fixed position, were more the rule than the exception. The fighting temporarily took on more than a semblance of the orthodox forms of warfare. Lack of heavy equipment placed the anti-Treatyites at a distinct disadvantage and should have made them even more reticent to fight pitched battles along fixed lines. They had less expertise and training in this type of warfare than the National Army, and it forced them to fall further back on the defensive.

CHAPTER 1

THE EAST LIMERICK IRA

Bruff, Bruree and Kilmallock were part of the territory of the East Limerick Brigade of the IRA. During the War of Independence East Limerick outperformed its counterparts in Mid and West Limerick in terms of intensity of activity and successful military outcome. East Limerick also suffered the highest number of casualties. Of the forty-eight Limerick IRA men who were killed, twenty-two were East Limerick Brigade Volunteers. Crown forces also suffered heavy casualties. Donnchadh O'Hannigan of East Limerick was perhaps the most successful flying column commandant who went pro-Treaty.

Tensions between Republican and Crown forces in Limerick remained high during the Truce, and fire was exchanged on several occasions. General Sir Peter Strickland, who commanded the 6th Division of the British army in Munster, urged his superiors to consider resuming military action on an extended scale if the IRA did not curtail its activities.[1]

The transition the IRA had to make, from secret, self-contained guerrilla organisation during the War of Independence, to peacetime activities during the Truce, accentuated problems of discipline and control.[2] There was regular open drilling. Volunteers, including men who had been on the run, wore their uniforms and socialised openly in the city and towns. On 2 August 1921 Kilmallock railway station was raided by several men who took away parcels consigned from England to a local trader. They left an IRA receipt.[3] On 8 August IRA notices were posted up in Newcastlewest ordering public houses to close at 8 p.m. An IRA dance took place at Caherconlish school on 13 August at which Volunteers 'were drunk and brandished revolvers and automatics'.[4]

IRA GHQ was concerned about discipline and at the end of November 1921 ordered an inquiry into whether any Volunteers were involved in the apparent falsification of betting telegraphs at Kilmallock and the holding up of two post office officials who were in Kilmallock for an inquiry into the matter.[5] On the night of 16 November armed men had seized papers from the officials which apparently contained proof of telegram betting and ordered them to leave Kilmallock on the first train in the morning.[6] The Kilmallock postmaster, Mr Bleech, received a threatening letter in relation to the planned inquiry on 19 November.[7]

Despite the concern of both Strickland and Volunteer GHQ, however, the East Limerick IRA stepped up its activities. On 14 December 1921 two Thurles RIC men were ambushed by the IRA while attending a coursing meeting in Kilmallock. Constable Thomas Enright was shot dead when leaving Clery's Hotel in Lord Edward Street, and Constable Tierney was seriously wounded.[8] East Limerick Brigade flying column Volunteer Maurice Meade claimed that Enright was:

... particularly active and bitter against our men, on one occasion bombing some of our captured men. For this we decided he should pay the death penalty. No opportunity to carry this out had arisen until the Truce occurred but when we saw him at the coursing match, even though the Truce was then in operation, we agreed to shoot him and we did so that night.

The Volunteers used a car which they had seized from a Lieutenant Brown, the British army intelligence officer in Kilmallock. Brown had himself previously seized the car from Tomás Malone, one of the leading Volunteers in the East Limerick Brigade. Malone and Brown actually socialised together during the coursing meeting.[9] Brown had been the subject of much Volunteer attention during the War of Independence but managed to survive several attacks. Sergeant James Maguire, who was killed in Kilmallock in March 1921, had been Brown's RIC liaison.

Constable Lauchlin McEdward was shot dead by the IRA at Garryowen in Limerick city on 17 February 1922; this and the killing of Enright, were the most glaring examples of local autonomy and resistance to central authority by the IRA. While the killing of Enright was motivated by vengeance, these incidents should also perhaps be viewed in the context of the belief that if the British could have been provoked into hostile action there would have been a chance of re-uniting the IRA.

Of the East Limerick Brigade staff at the time of the Truce, only Tomás Malone took the anti-Treaty side. Liam Hayes, who was also a staff member, voted in favour of the Treaty in Dáil Éireann. Despite the fact that a number of former East Limerick

Brigade office holders who were in prison at the time of the Truce sided against the Treaty when they were released, East Limerick was the only brigade in the 2nd Southern Division to throw the bulk of its weight behind the Treaty.

A number of battalions outside of East Limerick also took the pro-Treaty side, however. Mid Limerick had a majority of anti-Treatyites but a significant minority of pro Treatyites. Dick O'Connell's 4th Mid Limerick Battalion was mainly pro-Treaty, and 70 per cent of Seán Carroll's 2nd Battalion took the pro-Treaty side, even though Carroll himself was one of the most prominent anti-Treaty leaders in the region. The Mid Limerick Brigade quartermaster, Captain Seán Hurley, tried to organise these groups into a pro-Treaty unit but there were often divisions within individual units.

A Free State South Western Command report of 22 August 1922 on Mid Limerick commented that:

> We have had trouble with this brigade owing to the inactivity of our troops there, and the activity of the Irregulars under Seán Carroll. The object of Seán Carroll has been to break our road and rail communications with Dublin and with this in view, he keeps a column working in the Birdhill-Castleconnell areas.[10]

Members of the Free State army were frequently arrested in Carroll's territory: however, his relationship with Liam Forde was acrimonious and he eventually transferred his unit to Tipperary.

West Limerick was predominantly anti-Treaty. Brigadier

Garret McAuliffe explained to Ernie O'Malley that 'our Bde [Brigade] stayed firm but some of the junior officers went F/S [Free State]'.[11] West Limerick was even busier than Carroll's area early in the war, but was overrun by Free State troops by the end of the year. In the middle of October 1922 one anti-Treatyite informed the 1st Southern Division of a conversation he had with McAuliffe:

> I was speaking to the O/C West Limerick Brigade, who stated that owing to enemy activity in his brigade and the arrest of practically all his staff he was unable to attend to communications.[12]

Despite having an experienced anti-Treaty force, County Limerick was neutralised as a threat to the Free State early in 1923. In February 1923 Ernie O'Malley noted that:

> West Limerick is attached as a battalion to Cork no. 4 brigade. There are none of our men armed or active in this area. I am unable to give enemy strength but some of the towns are strongly held by him.[13]

The presence of a significant pro-Treaty IRA element in Limerick was crucial in the defeat of the anti-Treaty IRA. It meant that the Free State knew both the countryside and their opponents.

In Kilmallock two officers of the local Volunteer Company, Captain Michael Fitzgibbon and Second Lieutenant John O'Donnell, took the pro-Treaty side and joined the newly formed Free State army. Michael Mortell, a former captain of the company and a member of the East Limerick Brigade flying column, also went pro-Treaty. The majority of the Kilmallock Company, however, took the anti-Treaty side.

The company was reorganised in the spring of 1922 and new officers were elected: Captain Seán Hayes, First Lieutenant James Chamberlain, Second Lieutenant Michael Walsh, Intelligence Officer Daniel O'Brien, Quartermaster Tim Tierney and Adjutant Patrick Downes. Seán T. O'Riordan, who was battalion commandant during the War of Independence, had been released from prison in October 1921 and now became O/C of the East Limerick Brigade IRA. O'Riordan's predecessor as brigadier, Donnchadh O'Hannigan, had taken charge of the 4th Southern Division of the new National Army. James Chamberlain later changed his allegiance from anti-Treaty to pro-Treaty, left the IRA and took up a job in Dublin.

The majority of the neighbouring Ballingaddy Company took the Republican side after the Treaty split. Volunteers from the townlands of Ballygibba, Knocksouna and Tankardstown in the west of the parish were members of the Bruree Company. The division in the Bruree Company seems to have been between those who continued in the post-Truce IRA and those who took no active part in the Civil War – very few if any of the Bruree Volunteers went pro-Treaty.

As the dispute over the Treaty became more fractious, the building at Gortboy, Kilmallock, which the RIC had been using as a barracks, and that part of the Kilmallock Workhouse which had been in the hands of the British army, were occupied by members of the Kilmallock Company and by members of IRA companies from surrounding districts. An officer representing Donnchadh O'Hannigan subsequently invited these units to join the army of the Provisional Government. Those who were not willing to join the National Army withdrew from the garrisons. With the exception of one part of the workhouse, which remained in anti-Treaty hands, these important positions were now held by Free State forces.

A pattern of hostile incidents between the two sides emerged and continued until mid-July when the Civil War found its way to Kilmallock. At that point, the Republicans evacuated their wing of the workhouse to facilitate an attack by their colleagues on the rest of the building. Around midnight on 13–14 July the anti-Treaty IRA surrounded and captured the workhouse from the Free State army, after a determined attack forced the defenders to surrender.[14]

CHAPTER 2

THE BRUFF-BRUREE-KILMALLOCK TRIANGLE

Accounts of the Civil War by anti-Treaty veterans, such as Mossie Harnett of the West Limerick Brigade, occasionally attribute their military defeat to the fact that their hearts were not fully in the struggle.[1] There is some evidence to suggest that this interpretation is sustainable as a factor in the battle for Kilmallock. Connie Neenan of Cork had a dispiriting experience in Limerick before, during and after the battles for Limerick city and Kilmallock. It was characterised by indecision and uncertainty on the part of anti-Treaty military leaders:

When our brigade in Cork heard of the attack on the Four Courts we met straightaway. We decided to reinforce Limerick. My party was stopped at Buttevant but we reached Broadford in Limerick the first night. We were caught there between two Free State posts. With me were a number that I recall. Corney Sullivan and a lad named Spillane. Next thing the shooting started and Spillane fell. We all lay prone. I could see his rifle had dropped away from him. He died in five minutes. That was the start of it for us. We went from there to Rathkeale where we met Liam Lynch. We moved on to Adare; we captured a post there. Then we arrived in Limerick. We lost a couple of great lads there ... Who ordered us to leave Limerick? Well, it is hard to say. Tom Kelleher says our position was a strong one and Limerick was of crucial importance to us. He blames Deasy and Lynch – I am not sure ... We were in a tight situation. In the end we had no chance against them. Retreat became inevitable. My strongest complaint is that we were ordered out at an early hour of the evening when it was still daylight. That made it all the harder. The retreat when it came, resembled a stampede. We were the last to leave the new barracks, it was a scene of chaos; everyone was gone. We were so hungry that I went out and stole a loaf of bread. But then, we Republicans as you can see from Ernie O'Malley, were hopeless at looking after the commissariat. You would think that we had never heard of Napoleon's diktat – an army marches on its stomach. And so we fell back through Patrickswell, Adare, finally ending up in Buttevant about four o'clock in the morning. We felt hopelessly disillusioned and disheartened. The whole flaming struggle seemed to be leading nowhere. They captured our men; held them and later shot some of them. We captured their men, sometimes twice over, and had to let them go. We had nowhere to put them, no arrangements. No one now had the heart to fight.[2]

Neenan's comments on the IRA's inability to hold prisoners are particularly revealing and this failing was highlighted by Free State propagandists upon the release of Commandant Liam Hayes and Brigadier Dick O'Connell in early August:

They were seized some time ago by the mutineers who have now apparently discovered that they are unable to retain those whom they have carried into captivity. It is the beginning of the end.[3]

Another Corkman who was fighting with the anti-Treaty forces in Limerick at this point was Tom Kelleher, commandant general of the 1st Southern Division. Kelleher, like Neenan, was highly critical of his superiors on the anti-Treaty side and their failure to take the initiative in the war:

It is my personal opinion that Liam Lynch and Liam Deasy were simply not up to it, but neither was our headquarters staff in Dublin. We were allowed to fragment in the countryside when we should have throttled the Staters in the early months of 1922. Tom [Barry] hearkened back to his Bruff period of February/March when, with sections of the West Cork column, he was given the impossible task – from a manpower point of view – of preventing the seizure of that part of the country.

It was not the quality of the fighting men on the Republican side which held them back, according to Kelleher, but the failure of their leaders to allow them to fight:

In Limerick we had plenty of good fighters. The Staters were not numerous. Yet attacks were not pressed when they could have been. At Bruff we were throwing rifle grenades on top of the barracks. We now had it on target. They would have surrendered in a short time. At that moment a messenger came with a note, you are urgently required, it said. We called off our attack. I thought something big was on. What was it. We were being disbanded into small and ineffective groups. I could not see the sense of it … So the attack was stopped and we moved away. It was typical of the stop-go tactics of the Republican Army on the run-up to the Civil War. But there was no stop-go on the Free State side, they were all go, man.[4]

Mick Murphy and Jamie Managhan, both officers of Cork No. 1, were also contemptuous of the policy of retreat. Murphy commented that 'we came back to Buttevant, but why we did not know', while Managhan recalled how 'There was pandemonium … our men from Limerick were completely demoralised.'[5] The loss of Limerick city undoubtedly resulted in a huge blow to morale for Republicans. It was also a great boost to Provisional Government forces in the East Limerick Brigade area, where they had been under considerable pressure from the IRA: 'owing to the evacuation of Limerick by our Forces,' Adjutant-General Con Moloney reported to General Ernie O'Malley, O/C 2nd Southern Division, 'the enemy in E[ast]/Limerick area got a new lease of life.'[6]

On the Free State side, the Kilmallock area was taken in hand by Donnchadh O'Hannigan and W. R. E. Murphy. It was Murphy's responsibility to draft the operational orders for the offensives Eoin O'Duffy planned to secure County Limerick for the Free State. Murphy's main focus of attention became centred on East Limerick, where the Republican forces had fortified themselves around Bruff, Bruree and Kilmallock. Murphy, conscious of the inexperience and probable brittleness of many of the National Army troops, and hoping to keep casualties to a minimum, wished to avoid direct head-on assaults as much as possible and so drafted his plans with the intention of turning the Republican positions through flanking manoeuvres. The number of troops initially available to O'Duffy and Murphy was 2,500, but they had to be distributed throughout the South Western Command.

Initially, the most that could be spared for any particular operation was 800: less than the number of Republicans in East Limerick.[7] However, there were eventually well over 1,000 National Army soldiers involved in the battle for Kilmallock. It has been suggested that Michael Collins and Richard Mulcahy formulated Free State strategy while O'Duffy and Murphy were tactically reliant on sheer weight of numbers.[8]

The implications of the fall of Limerick city, in tandem with the fall of Waterford at the same time in the east, prematurely convinced the pro-Treaty leadership that the war was nearly over, as the whole of the Munster Republic seemed to be on the verge of collapse. Moloney outlined the situation to O'Malley:

You remember I told you we had closed around Thurles. Well through a series of delays and bungles our troops had to withdraw from the immediate vicinity of that town and operate in Clonmel in front of Line: Tipperary, Cashel, Clonmel, Carrick-on-Suir, Waterford.

Some one got 'Breeze up' the other day and Clonmel Barracks was ordered to be burned, fortunately as HQ officers arrived on the spot before this piece of work had been completed [*sic*]. Tipperary and Cashel Barracks (More 'Breeze up') are I understand also destroyed. However, a GHQ officer has managed to rally things a bit there 'The efficient 2nd southern'.[9]

Moloney was expecting a Free State army attack on Waterford or Carrick-on-Suir, but he was hopeful that should the IRA take the war to the Free State in the south-east they could sustain a prolonged campaign of resistance to the Treaty: 'if we can get the initiative in these areas I think we can carry on indefinitely'.[10] His hopes for progress in the south-east were to be dashed, however. Waterford, which had been occupied by around 200 IRA Volunteers since the start of the war, fell to pro-Treaty forces on 21 July, the same day as Limerick. The Waterford men were not as well equipped with guns and ammunition as their anti-Treaty comrades in Limerick. Neither, it seems, were they as committed to the cause, desertion being frequent and leading officers resigning as the prospect of civil war became a reality.

In yet another example of flawed Republican policy, there was a lack of co-operation between Waterford and the Republican strongholds of Cork and Tipperary, with the result that the city did not receive sufficient support from those quarters. The defence of the city was half-hearted and incompetent and the pro-Treaty success much easier than might have been expected. As in Dublin and Limerick, Republicans came under fire from Free State artillery, but Dublin and Limerick had not capitulated in the way Waterford did. That city was a microcosm of the wider Civil War in that it demonstrated the reluctance of Republicans to fight, or at least fight to the bitter end in conventional battles, and it showed that pro-Treaty successes often had more to do with anti-Treaty failures than Free State strategy.[11]

After 21 July, then, all the major towns and connecting roads between Waterford city in the east and Limerick city in the west were in pro-Treaty hands, with O'Duffy at the reins. Clonmel and Carrick-on-Suir, the principal towns in south Tipperary, had been under assured anti-Treaty control in early July, but Republicans there seemed to succumb to inaccurate rumours about the imminent arrival of Provisional Government forces and lost confidence. Clonmel and Carrick were evacuated. Liam Lynch's Limerick–Waterford defensive demarcation line of the Munster Republic, which had been somewhat fanciful and which Calton Younger decried as 'always something of a joke', no longer existed in any way, shape or form.[12] A planned Republican counter-attack in Waterford never materialised and the war was more or less finished there, but the same cannot be said of Limerick.

Any expectation that Republican resistance throughout the entire south would crumble almost immediately after 21 July was unrealistic. O'Duffy was sorely frustrated, initially because the Free State victory in Limerick city was countered in the short term by the considerable concentration of Republican forces in County Limerick. When the IRA abandoned Limerick city, the Free State held only Rockbarton and Bruff in the county. This was nearly a month after the Civil War started in Dublin but, aside from Limerick city, most of Munster was still under the control of the anti-Treaty IRA with only isolated units of Free State troops established in cities and towns. Bruff was one of these places, where about twenty pro-Treatyites were ensconced in the old RIC barracks. Rockbarton House was also occupied by Free Staters and the 4th Southern Division of the National Army set up their HQ there. O'Duffy estimated that the anti-Treatyites, with 2,030 rifles in total in Limerick, 'still outnumber us by 727 Rifles'.[13] The Provisional Government experienced much greater difficulties in attaining control of County Limerick, particularly east Limerick, than they had in taking Limerick city.

Republican control of the Bruff-Bruree-Kilmallock triangle, and the rest of County Limerick, could only be temporary, however, but they did manage to delay the pro-Treaty advance to the south for over two weeks. These two weeks had significant consequences for the geographical and military context and progression of the Civil War thereafter. Shortly after Kilmallock fell, the majority of Republicans who continued the fight were effectively penned back into Cork and Kerry.

Some of the difficulties encountered by the IRA around Kilmallock were outlined in a request to the 1st Southern Division on 16 July:

> Supplies very scarce here – no meat whatsoever. A daily supply is necessary. Some bedding also necessary. Philpot the QM has list of requirements. Am about to proceed to Ashill [*sic*] Towers with view to taking it over.[14]

As anti-Treaty forces naturally gravitated towards Kilmallock, many Cork and Kerry men who had been in Limerick city set themselves up in Ash Hill Towers, a large house which became the local Republican HQ. *Sgéal Chatha Luimnighe*, in its typically blustering and exaggerated fashion, described how the building 'overlooks the town and practi[cally] commands every street'.[15]

Michael Francis O'Donovan O'Connor of Cork, an IRA Volunteer who wrote for the Republican-controlled *Cork Examiner* (he was known as Frank O'Connor during his post-war literary career, as he will be referred to here), found himself in the 'pseudo-Gothic castle' of Ash Hill Towers:

> In the long Gothic hall there were fifty or sixty men at either side of the long trestle tables in the candle-light, their rifles slung over their shoulders. The hall seemed to tremble with the flickering of the candles, and tusked and antlered heads peered down from the half-darkness as even they couldn't believe what they were seeing. Suddenly a young man sprang on a table with a rifle in his hand and sang …

The scene seems to have been one of surrealism more than optimism, however, and this sense of unreality, as far as O'Connor was concerned, extended outside Ash Hill Towers and pervaded Republican activity in the surrounding area:

> If only I had realised it, it was here that the genius of improvisation had taken complete charge. In Buttevant and Fermoy we had real barracks, complete with officers' messes; we had an armoured car – a most improbable-looking vehicle, like the plywood tank that captured a Chinese town where a friend was living, flying a large streamer that said 'Particularly Fierce

Tank'. We even had a Big Gun that had been made by a Dub-
liner who had brought it with him to Buttevant along with the
nine shells he had made for it and the tenth that was still in
the process of construction. But the front line was our pride
and joy. We had improvised almost everything else but never
a front line. The enemy were reported to be on the point of
attacking it, and in the library the local officers were hard at
work over their maps deciding which bridges to blow up in the
track of their advance.[16]

The armoured car was 'The River Lee' of the 1st Cork Brigade,
and according to IRA Volunteer Jamie Managhan, it 'cruised
around like a labourer's cottage'. The vehicle was actually a coal
lorry that had been fitted with armoured plates in Cork city
and was armed with two Lewis machine guns. Seán Murray,
of Cork No. 1 Brigade, thought that 'the men had no intention
of holding a line'. There may not have been any food on the
'long trestle tables' described by O'Connor because, in the words
of Murray, 'they had to scrounge for themselves'. Liam Deasy
admitted that the situation with supplies was so bad that they
had to demobilise men because they could not feed them.

An element of competition, if not necessarily hostility, was
evident between the Republican forces from various areas as
the problems of local particularism, which had occasionally
undermined IRA activity during the War of Independence, re-
emerged around Kilmallock. Logistical support and co-operation
between units from different counties was poor and unreliable.
Deasy's command included Volunteers from Limerick itself,
Cork and Kerry, all of whom had their own commanders. Patrick

O'Donnell of the East Limerick Brigade reported that his men 'refused to operate under Cork, as they would much prefer to operate in their own divisional area. They let our men down badly; it was impossible to get anything from them.'[17]

O'Connor echoed this theme of Cork/Limerick rivalry in the ranks of the anti-Treaty IRA when recalling his encounter in Buttevant with the 'angriest looking men [he had] ever seen':

> ... we're the Limerick Column ... We're after fighting our way down from Patrickswell, and when we got here the Corkmen had meat for their breakfast and we had none. Tell [Deasy] if the Limerick men don't get meat there'll be mutiny.

Deasy, apparently well used to this type of complaint, 'took the news of the possible mutiny as calmly as he'd taken the news of the expected assault on the front line'.[18] While Deasy, as O/C 1st Southern Division, was 'more or less i/c operations', Seán Moylan's official role was director of operations.[19]

To review the situation during the opening days of the battle for Kilmallock, then, Republicans enjoyed territorial dominance in east Limerick – possession of the town was ninth-tenths of the law – and had the advantage in the quantity of men and level of firepower in the immediate area. As long as they occupied it, the hilly terrain better served the purposes of the defenders.

It was estimated that there were 500 Republicans in Kilmallock and another 1,000 further south in Buttevant, Co. Cork. They also had the better calibre troops and some of the most proven campaigners from the War of Independence, among them Deasy and Moylan. O'Duffy's assessment was that 'practically the entire forces of the Irregulars are arraigned against us', among them the most active and most efficient Cork and Kerry Republicans, who were some of the best fighting men on either side of the conflict.[20]

Many of the Free State soldiers, on the other hand, were raw recruits, inexperienced and unreliable. O'Duffy was scathing in his assessment of the quality of troops and officers at his disposal. Reflecting on the battle for Kilmallock, he later told National Army Chief of Staff, General Richard Mulcahy that:

> We had to get work out of a disgruntled, undisciplined and cowardly crowd. Arms were handed over wholesale to the enemy, sentries were drunk at their Posts, and when a whole garrison was put in clink owing to insubordination, etc., the garrison sent to replace them often turned out to be worse, and the Divisional, Brigade, Battalion, and Company officers were in many cases, no better than the Privates. To get value out of these the Command Staff had to work very hard – 18 hours out of 24 ... as there was always fear we might lose some of the posts through treachery, as actually happened on two occasions.[21]

The reinforcements from the Curragh Reserve seemed to fare little better. The view of Colonel Commandant Tom Keogh, formerly a member of Michael Collins' Squad, and now a leader of the Dublin Guard, was that 'The Reserve are absolutely worthless, at least 200 of them never handled a rifle before'. O'Duffy also reported, 'Half of them are now in clink, or have deserted altogether.'[22] W. R. E. Murphy had to personally quell an incipient mutiny amongst one unit over the dismissal of an incompetent officer. He apparently assembled the troops in question and threatened to shoot the first person to disobey orders. On another occasion he despatched an officer to report on the condition of a garrison only to find that they were all in bed. They were all arrested and Murphy had them put in cells in the New Barracks.[23]

While the anti-Treatyites were experiencing problems with morale, logistics, supplies and unity, the pro-Treatyites, despite the strong and clear leadership provided by O'Duffy and Murphy, could not immediately capitalise on this dissension and compensate for their inexperience because they were outnumbered and outgunned. As well as having more rifles, the Republicans had three improvised armoured cars, a mortar and heavy machine guns.[24]

However, the Free State forces held the trump card of Limerick city, from where they could consolidate and reinforce. They were also able to draft in more battle-hardened troops over time as well as the artillery which the Republicans lacked. O'Duffy, however, even on the eve of the conquest of Kilmallock, was still not satisfied with the performance of his troops, and he continued to complain about the lack of resources at his disposal. On 4 August he wrote:

We are operating in large areas with nothing better than a Rifle. I estimate that the Irregulars have 4 Lewis Guns in this Command for our one. In Limerick City at the moment there is not a single Lewis Gun ... As regards Rifles, the last rifle is distributed and I have none for the recruits coming in.

There were neither touring cars nor motorcycles available to the Free Staters and O'Duffy pleaded for transport facilities, as well as increased supplies: 'As it is, our troops have to scrounge on the countryside. This leads towards undiscipline and is unfair to the people.'[25]

There was doubtless an element of exaggeration to O'Duffy's dismissal of the ability of his forces, but these internal National Army communications provide a much more accurate image of how he judged his men than the press releases designed for public consumption. In a statement issued on Friday 28 July, O'Duffy pronounced that the anti-Treatyites in east Limerick, whatever their status, were no match for his Free State army:

> The best fighting material the irregulars can muster is ranged against us. Having concentrated all their forces from Munster on the Kilmallock frontier, they have the advantage in quantity, but in quality the advantage is very much with us.[26]

Deasy, like O'Duffy, had grave concerns about some of the men under his command. 'Laxity,' according to Deasy, was 'characteristic of our forces':

> While I was carrying out a late evening inspection of the Kilmallock line I came to an important cross-roads on the main Limerick-Charleville road. The defence of this cross-roads was vital to us since it could prevent an attack coming in from Limerick on our flank. I found only one man on duty there. He told me that six others had gone to Charleville for a drink. I found them drinking in the late Seán O'Brien's bar. The only

excuse or explanation they offered was that they were tired and weary of the long protective duty and had come to town for a bit of a break. All I could do was order them to return to their … home unit and I then arranged for a more reliable replacement from our reserve force at Buttevant.[27]

The reality of the situation was most likely that neither of the two opposing forces met all the requirements of a standing army. In some respects the engagement represented the clash of unevenly trained combinations that had been cobbled together. Many of the men were not properly prepared for combat. Desertion and transfer of allegiance were not uncommon, although that was by no means unique to the Civil War. At times, coordinated action on any large scale proved beyond the capabilities of either side, particularly the anti-Treatyites. The National Army may have been slightly more competent in terms of military strategy because of its more formal structure. Both sides were initially confident, however, but local momentum had been with the Republicans since the middle of July and this trend continued for the first week or so of the battle for Kilmallock.

During the battle for Limerick city there had been a number of significant shifts in the balance of power in favour of the anti-Treaty IRA in east Limerick. Republicans had a remarkably successful day on Wednesday 12 July, when they managed to capture the whole pro-Treaty brigade staff of East Limerick at Caherconlish, numbering forty-seven. The prisoners were taken to Tipperary Barracks.[28] Various sources give differing details on what exactly happened at Caherconlish. Some name

Commandant Peter Kearney of the 3rd West Cork Brigade as being in charge of the anti-Treaty force, others Seán Moylan. The anti-Treaty column may have been 'moving to hold the Tipp.-Limerick lines' or heading from Cork to assist their comrades in Limerick city or even heading to Waterford from Limerick. In any case, the position was seized and the Republicans took a number of Free State officers prisoner, including Dick O'Connell, commander of the Free State forces in the Mid Limerick Brigade area; '[Liam] Hayes TD Bde O/C', who, in both his political and military capacities, was one of the leading pro-Treaty figures in east Limerick; and five others, among them Joe Graham and John Joe O'Brien, who were both experienced campaigners from the War of Independence.[29] Just under a month later O'Connell and Hayes, 'along with practically all the Limerick officers who had been forcibly detained by the irregulars for some time past [had] been released'.[30]

Republicans also took control of Kilmallock at this stage, beginning their attack on the Free State garrison there at approximately 9.30 p.m. on Wednesday 12 July:[31] 'the troops at the Union barracks were cut off from communication with the outside. The garrison of forty-nine men … held out for forty-eight hours and finally yielded, having only a small supply of ammunition left.'[32] Republicans claimed to have taken 150 prisoners in the process and 'a large number of rifles etc., fell into our hands. A party of Free State troops on the way to relieve Kilmallock, were put to flight by our forces.'[33]

An awkward peace, interrupted by some minor altercations, had prevailed between the pro- and anti-Treaty forces occupying positions in Kilmallock since the beginning of 1922. Free

State General Séamas Hogan felt that it had been an error to hold Caherconlish and Kilmallock because they were weak positions with weak garrisons, and on 15 July he reported to GHQ that the position of the National Army in both east and west Limerick was 'not good':

> Flying columns from each (East Limerick and West Limerick) are passing through and Commdt Hannigan [*sic*] does not seem strong enough to cope with them. He is short of rifles, and until he has more will not be able to check movements to and from Cork. I have found it rather difficult to wean Hannigan from the idea of holding posts in East Limerick. I instructed Commdt Hannigan only to hold posts that could resist any attack.[34]

If the situation looked somewhat bleak for the Free State forces in east Limerick at this stage, it looked, superficially at least, much more promising for their anti-Treaty rivals. On 18 July Con Moloney sent a memo to Ernie O'Malley, reviewing the situation in the Munster Republic. Republican GHQ had recently shifted further south again, from Clonmel to Fermoy, but Moloney was in an upbeat mood. He was still enthusiastic about the situation in Limerick city, where he judged things to be 'progressing magnificently' and making up for 'shortcomings in other areas'. This was probably not a wholly unrealistic assessment of the situation on 18 July – circumstances were about to change dramatically with the arrival of Free State field guns in the city, however. Deasy, according to Moloney, was quite bullish about his prospects in east Limerick:

First Southern Troops are operating in E[ast]/Limerick Brigade area and have captured Kilmallock Barracks: 22 Rifles, 150 men, very little .303. At present a fight is in progress around Bulgadin Cross on a front of about four miles. [Donnchadh O']Hannigan is i/c operations on the Enemy side. They number about 400. [Liam] Deasy is more or less i/c operations for us with about half the number of Troops at his disposal. He is confident of success, as any time both forces have met in this area, 'the enemy ran away'.[35]

Moloney's reference to Deasy as being 'more or less' in charge of operations points to a level of uncertainty in the overall Republican command structure in the area and to a lack of cohesion which had important consequences as the battle for Kilmallock unfolded.

The unreliability of the pro-Treaty forces enormously encouraged the Republicans and this pattern was further in evidence at Bruff when some members of the Free State garrison there deserted to the Republican side on 20 July.[36] Both the pro- and anti-Treaty forces recognised the significance of Bruff and Bruree as gateways to Kilmallock. There was considerable fighting in Bruff and Bruree in the last ten days of July, with both towns being taken and retaken by one side and then the other. Neither side was initially able to deliver a knockout blow to the enemy, and the pendulum swayed back and forth.

The action started in the early hours of Thursday 20 July, when Republican forces launched an assault designed to take possession of Bruff and when some of the Free State garrison in the town deserted and converted to the anti-Treaty cause.

A Republican prisoner taken near Kilmallock, 22 July 1922.
(Courtesy of the National Library of Ireland)

Ash Hill Towers. *(Courtesy of Limerick Museum)*

Devon Castle, Newcastlewest. *(Courtesy of Limerick Museum)*

Injured soldier being attended to by National Army medics near Kilmallock, 25 July 1922. *(Courtesy of the National Library of Ireland)*

General Eoin O'Duffy, probably in Cruise's Hotel, 27 July 1922. *(Courtesy of the National Library of Ireland)*

National troops in Bruff, 27 July 1922. *(Courtesy of the National Library of Ireland)*

Major General W. R. E. Murphy, 27 January 1923.
(Courtesy of the National Library of Ireland)

National Army medics at work – probably in Bruff – 27 July 1922.
(Courtesy of the National Library of Ireland)

Donnchadh O'Hannigan, O/C
4th Southern Division, National
Army.

Liam Deasy, O/C 1st
Southern Division IRA.

THE LATE GENERAL LIAM LYNCH
CHIEF OF STAFF I.R.A.

Liam Lynch, IRA chief of staff.

Seán Moylan, O/C North Cork (No. 2) Brigade IRA.

Con Moloney, adjutant-general 2nd Southern Division IRA.

Commandant Tom Flood, Dublin Guard, National Army.

A number of these men may actually have taken part in the IRA attack. Tom Kelleher of Cork told Uinseann MacEoin, 'I had three deserters, complete with uniforms, and they were prepared to fight with us.'[37]

Kelleher had planned the operation with another West Cork veteran, Tom Barry. Acting in liaison with local Republicans, who had a more intimate knowledge of the area, the Cork and Kerry men ascertained that the Free Staters in Bruff 'sent out a big column every night ... and they return each morning at daybreak'. Based on this intelligence, they were hopeful that they could take Bruff 'without firing a shot'. This was an unrealistic goal because the barracks in Bruff was an imposing building which dominated the immediate town and offered visibility over a wider area. Its entrance was reinforced with sandbags and barbed wire, most of the windows were fitted with steel plates, and thick loopholes provided cover against small-arms fire.

The encounter began when Free State officers on an inspection patrol on the outskirts of Bruff ran into a group of more than thirty IRA men who emerged from the cover of a house. The National Army contingent, 'being hopelessly outnumbered, retreated to the barracks, and succeeded in gaining their objective'.[38] There were twenty-six anti-Treatyites in the column which entered Bruff, according to Kelleher, including four in Free State uniform – the three recent additions from the pro-Treaty side and Kelleher himself. Later on that day Republican Field GHQ at Ash Hill Towers reported to O/C Southern Division on the progress of the Bruff operation:

At 3 a.m. this morning columns 6 and 7 entered Bruff and took up positions on the east, west and south sides of the Free State barracks. As they were entering a sharp engagement took place, in which Comdt Tom O'Connor of the 6th Battn Kerry No. 2 brigade got seriously wounded through the left shoulder ... the enemy is practically surrounded.[39]

The Freeman's Journal of 25 July described the fighting: 'torrents of machine-gun and rifle fire, punctuated by the explosion of hand grenades broke the stillness of the morning'. The *Limerick Chronicle* of the same day referred to 'a heavy attack' carried out by 'Irregulars' from Kilmallock, Buttevant and Charleville but reassured the public that 'The National forces had made elaborate preparations for defence.'

Kelleher gave a colourful participant's account of events to MacEoin:

A sentry outside the barracks had the presence of mind to rush inside and slam the door. I could have shot him in the back without any difficulty but I did not. His friends are inside and if I shoot this fellow in the back they will fire out and we stand a bad chance. There was a porthole on the left. I stuck in my Thompson and sprayed the yard with bullets. When I looked around there was no one beside me only a young fellow of about seventeen. Come here, I whispered; we will get away by passing underneath the windows. Meanwhile, the column had moved up to the right. There was one fellow there, Donoghue from West Cork, who had been in the British Army and who knew all about rifle grenades. He had a rifle, its cup and a grenade on top of it. He had two or three bags of bombs.

'We'll take this in a short time.'

I moved up beside him.

'You are too near,' says he.

'Why, why,' says I. Ah, some of the cartridges are not reliable: and when they are not reliable they can splinter in all directions.

We got the range, and the grenades were already exploding inside the building when the word came. I told you already a while back, you are wanted urgently in another place. So the attack was stopped and we moved away.[40]

The fact that the IRA had been equipped with a Thompson machine gun and explosives illustrates that it was indeed 'a heavy attack'. It seems also that the Free Staters had not only made 'elaborate preparations for defence' but had mounted dogged resistance. At one stage a member of the garrison apparently dashed out of the barracks, on to the street, and threw an unexploded grenade back in the direction from where it had come.[41]

The objective of the anti-Treaty units had clearly been to seize control of the town. They occupied the Munster and Leinster Bank, and the National Bank, as well as adjoining cottages. The attack was sustained and while it was ongoing other Republican forces were active in a supporting role in the surrounding area: 'No. 5 column is keeping Rockbarton engaged so as to keep off reinforcements from that side.' The fighting in Bruff continued until after 10 a.m. on Friday 21 July, at which point 'a calm set in and the Irregulars made towards Rockbarton with the evident intention of attacking the National garrison' there.[42] According to the *Limerick Chronicle*, however, 'they were intercepted by a body of National troops and driven in a westerly direction' before they could reach Rockbarton.[43]

Some families had fled Bruff during the fighting and there had been one civilian fatality. William Dunworth, a buyer at Messrs Todd & Co. Ltd in Limerick, was driving in the direction of Bruff when he inadvertently found himself in the middle of an engagement between pro- and anti-Treaty forces at the Pike, between Grange and Bruff. Dunworth got caught in the line of fire and was shot dead.[44]

The Republicans' decision to break off the attack and withdraw from Bruff was the one that had so frustrated Tom Kelleher and exemplified for him the counter-productive tactics of the anti-Treaty leadership. Con Moloney explained the commanders' rationale to Ernie O'Malley on 25 July:

> The enemy in this area was completely surrounded and capture was only a matter of very short time, but owing to the evacuation of Limerick by our Forces, the enemy in E[ast]/Limerick area got a new lease of life. Bruff Barracks was within a few hours of capture when the attack had to be called off, owing to evacuation of Limerick …[45]

'However,' continued Moloney, 'we have the whips [*sic*] hand in this area again.'

Shortly after midnight on 20–21 July the anti-Treatyite garrison which had held the New Barracks in Limerick city evacuated in a convoy of cars along the main Cork road through

Ballinacurra, which at that stage was the only route available for a mechanised retreat to the south and west, in the direction of Bruff, Bruree and Kilmallock. A rearguard provided cover in the form of intensive machine-gun fire as they left the outskirts of the city. They stopped only briefly, and at intervals of a few miles, 'to fell trees across the road, plant landmines and demolish bridges with explosives to slow any Free State troops advancing behind them'.[46] They fell back to the Bruff-Bruree-Kilmallock triangle, where they established defensive positions in anticipation of an onslaught from the Free State army, which would be forthcoming as soon as they had consolidated their control of Limerick city, reorganised and reinforced their troops, and built up their supplies. The retreating Republicans came under heavy machine-gun fire as they left the city but went largely unchallenged by the few Provisional Government forces in their path as they drove through the countryside, save for at Crossagalla, where an IRA Volunteer called Slattery was reportedly killed.[47]

In his 25 July memorandum to O'Malley, Moloney detailed a number of engagements that had occurred over the preceding two days and in which the enemy was 'completely routed':

At 4.30 this morning 23 July 1922 an armoured car with 27 of our men encountered a party of Free State troops advancing towards Kilmallock, on Bruff-Kilmallock road. After a short engagement the enemy retreated leaving two armed prisoners in our hands.

At 7.30 a.m. one of our Columns holding Bruree-Kilmallock road engaged enemy party advancing on Kilmallock direction, a short engagement resulted in the enemy retreating leaving one dead and two armed prisoners in our hands.

The same column entered a house near by and captured a further five armed Free Staters, without a fight.

At 2 p.m. 23 July 1922 we got information that there was a party of Free Staters between Kilmallock and Charleville. We sent an armoured car and 25 men to engage this Party. We came on the enemy near Thomastown. Enemy retreated to Farmer's House on road side. We weren't strong enough at the time to attack as a further party of enemy had engaged us. We kept up an intermittent fire, and awaited re-inforcements. These arrived at 8 p.m. We immediately attacked the house in which the enemy were and after 1 hour's fight we forced a surrender.

Result we captured:

26 Prisoners

26 Rifles – a quantity of ammunition

2 Revolvers

A phone message of yesterday's date states: 'Two engagements occurred yesterday in E[ast]/Limerick area resulting in our capturing 19 prisoners with rifles etc in the first case and 18 prisoners with rifles etc in the second engagement. The situation in this area is now well in hand'.[48]

Lynch, like Moloney, was optimistic at this point about anti-Treaty prospects on the Kilmallock front, 'after experience of East Limerick for last few days where we captured 76 armed prisoners and where enemy show no fight'.[49] Moloney referred to 'one dead' National Army soldier on 23 July but there do not seem to have been any fatalities on the Free State side until

24 July. These anti-Treaty successes are corroborated by contemporaneous daily Republican reports on operations in the Kilmallock area on 23 and 24 July, which state that fifty-eight prisoners, sixty rifles, 2,000 rounds of .303 ammunition along with sundry other war materials were captured with minimal Republican losses.[50]

They are further confirmed by O'Duffy's report to GHQ on 26 July of serious setbacks in the area. On 22 July thirty pro-Treatyites had been surprised and captured between Kilmallock and Bruff. The following day forty-seven men under a Commandant Cronin were captured after a five-hour engagement near Thomastown. O'Duffy laid the responsibility for this setback squarely on Cronin's shoulders because he had ignored orders that there should be no advance south of a certain point to the north of Kilmallock until the rest of Limerick had been cleared and further reinforcements were on the scene.[51]

Sgéal Chatha Luimnighe and the *Limerick Chronicle*, meanwhile, assiduously ignored these problems being encountered by the National Army and concentrated on whatever successes the Free State actually had, while simply inventing others:

> The triumph in Limerick has been swiftly followed by successes in the surrounding country. The centre of interest has shifted to the county, where the irregulars have evacuated Patrickswell, Croom, Manister, Rathmore Castle, Athlacca, Bruff, Hospital, and Pallasgreen. The Bishop of Limerick [Dr Denis Hallinan] visited the Headquarters of the National forces on Saturday and congratulated Comdt-Gen Michael Brennan on the successful outcome of the operations in the city.[52]

The vanguard of the National Army convoy travelling from Limerick city in the direction of Kilmallock had their southerly progress checked by a Republican force consisting of an armoured car of the 1st Cork Brigade, probably 'The River Lee', supported by men of the 5th Cork Brigade.[53] This encounter took place at Ballycullane Cross, about a mile north of Kilmallock on the Bruff Road, at 3.20 a.m. on Sunday 23 July. The IRA bulletin in *The Cork Examiner* of 25 July reported a 'sharp engagement': 'After a brief fight the Free State troops were defeated. One Free State soldier was killed and … four prisoners, four rifles … and a quantity of war equipment' were captured. The reference to a fatality is more than likely erroneous.

Less than ideal weather and road conditions did not favour a particularly rapid advance by either lorries or infantry. Likewise, the terrain, some of it dotted by high hedges and thick ditches, may well have better suited the purposes of defenders rather than attackers.

Also on Sunday 23 July, Frank O'Connor, on his first day of active service, and in an incident which had a positive conclusion for the IRA, was captured by Provisional Government troops. Along with two other anti-Treatyites, O'Connor was carrying despatches from Liam Deasy in Buttevant back to Kilmallock, when their car was stopped at Thomastown, which lies north of Charleville and south-west of Kilmallock. They were held temporarily at a Free State outpost in a nearby farmhouse. Just as the prisoners were being taken to lorries in the yard for transportation to Limerick, some of O'Connor's fellow Republicans surrounded the position and opened fire. An armoured car formed part of the attackers' arsenal and had an important psychological effect.

The Free Staters retired to the farmhouse with their prisoners and barricaded the window with bags of meal and a can of pitch. O'Connor suggested that one of the defenders, Sergeant Denis O'Mahony of Cork city, was killed. Again, this reported fatality seems unlikely, however, and further evidence to support his claim is not forthcoming. The Free State commander, a man named Mossie O'Brien, was wounded in the mouth, and was among those who subsequently switched from the pro-Treaty to the anti-Treaty side.

The garrison attempted to surrender when rifle grenades were used against the house but their signal went unobserved in the fading light, or was ignored, until O'Connor made his way under fire to his colleagues, while waving a white handkerchief, and established his identity. The surrender was accepted and he was put in charge of the prisoners who were taken back to Buttevant.[54] This was one of the Republican successes Con Moloney described to Ernie O'Malley.

Commandant Cronin's column was captured in the Thomastown area and, although the dates quoted in various reports do not correlate, there is a possibility that it was part of the action described by O'Connor. 'Many of them had no heart in the fighting,' wrote O'Connor in the IRA bulletin: 'The principal impression which the encounter with the Free Staters left in my mind was the utter lack of conviction that makes the Republicans fight like demons.'[55] While very often Republicans simply did not fight at all, they displayed admirable military tenacity in their activities in the Bruff-Bruree-Kilmallock triangle in the last week of July and inflicted a number of sobering defeats on the National Army. Meanwhile, on the day of O'Connor's capture and release (23 July), the Republicans once again turned their attention to Bruff, renewing their efforts to occupy it. On this occasion they completed the task successfully, even establishing a field hospital there. However, Free State forces re-established themselves there only a few days later.

The pro-Treaty forces suffered what was perhaps their most serious setback at this time at Ballingaddy on the evening of 24 July. Eoin Neeson, Calton Younger and Mainchín Seoighe all identified the National Army unit involved as being a section of the Dublin Guard under Commandant Tom Flood but it seems that it was actually a detachment of the column that had been led by Commandant Cronin.[56] Flood, however, had taken over command of field operations in the area by this point.

The troops were advancing towards Kilmallock from the direction of Effin when they stumbled upon an anti-Treaty outpost on a narrow, sunken road, surrounded by thick and high hedges, and became involved in a firefight near Pouladragoon Bridge, just south of the railway line. The official National Army report on the incident intimated that a number of troops were killed after they had been captured by the IRA:

> Lieut O'Leary and three men were captured by the enemy. Three of these men were found shot dead on the road this morning near the enemy post and it is believed they were shot after surrender.[57]

A first-hand account of the clash quoted by Neeson contradicts the Free State version of events:

It was about 3.30 p.m., and I was belly down in a ditch, the men stretched all round me. We had no field of fire as the hedges were too thick to see through and the bullets whizzing through them rendered any attempt to extend very hazardous. We were remarkably like rats in the proverbial cage. Twenty minutes later, however, a section succeeded in breaking off to the left through a gap in the rear, and, bit by bit, the pro-Treaty troops managed to withdraw under fire. The eye-witness noticed four soldiers crouched at the bottom of a bank waiting an opportunity to fire and had time to hope that the anti-Treaty machine gunners didn't see them bunched together, before a burst tore through them, killing three and fatally wounding the fourth. [this fourth man apparently survived].[58]

The following day, a war correspondent from *The Irish Times*, who seems to have been present during the fighting, accompanied the Red Cross party which, under a flag of truce, recovered three corpses. Surveying the scene, the reporter suggested that 'if the Irregulars had disposed their machine gun differently no one would have escaped'.

While the anti-Treatyites laid out the bodies and placed rosary beads in their folded hands, they did not move them from where they fell:

Two of them lay in the ditch where I had last seen them, and had noticed that they were too much bunched together. That machine gun had got into them after all. The third was in the flanking ditch, some fifty yards away, shot clean through the head.[59]

The three victims were Kerrymen: Corporal Cornelius Sullivan, Private Timothy Murphy and Private John Quirke.

Republicans vociferously denied wrongdoing at Ballingaddy, whereas the National Army report on the incident was somewhat tentative in its accusation. A 1924 GHQ report clarified that the deceased formed 'an advance or scouting party. They did not know the district, and came under fire from the Irregulars, in which they were killed'.[60]

On 25 July Lynch, reflecting on Republican military policy, suggested in a note to O'Malley that their forces should henceforth revert to guerrilla tactics exclusively, because they had been proving most successful and held out most promise for the future (although he identified the area around Kilmallock as an exception):

> Our military policy must be guerrilla tactics as in late war with common enemy, but owing to increased arms and efficiency of Officers and men, it can be waged more intensely. Guerrilla tactics are being carried out in all areas at the moment except 1st Southern Div; this area for some time can more effectively wage war by holding certain fronts. The enemy here will fail hopelessly in country unless he advances in mass formation and that would be too costly.

In light of what had been happening in east Limerick, Lynch was 'convinced of our open success in open country'.[61]

On 29 July Moloney informed O'Malley that 'We are holding an 8 mile front in Kilmallock-Bruff area.'[62] On 2 August Moloney suggested that 'Up to yesterday we have had the best of the operations', but he felt that the tide had started to turn against the Republicans: 'There will I fear be a big change there now as the enemy have been reinforced very considerably.'[63] Moloney was some days behind events, however, and the changes which he predicted were already well under way.

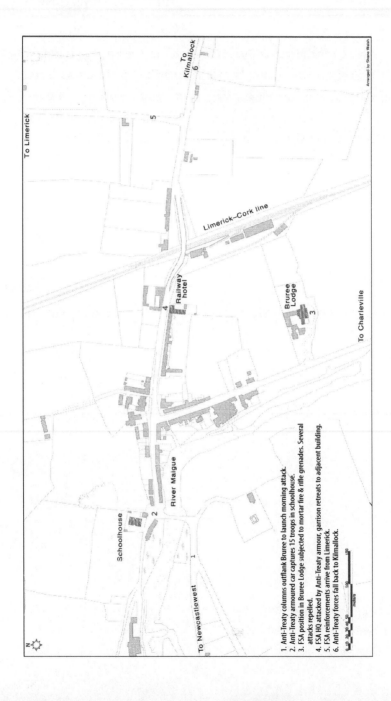

N

To Limerick

To Kilmallock

Limerick–Cork line

Railway hotel

Bruree Lodge

To Charleville

River Maigue

Schoolhouse

To Newcastlewest

1. Anti-Treaty columns outflank Bruree to launch morning attack.
2. Anti-Treaty armoured car captures 15 troops in schoolhouse.
3. FSA position in Bruree Lodge subjected to mortar fire & rifle grenades. Several
   attacks repelled.
4. FSA HQ attacked by Anti-Treaty armour, garrison retreats to adjacent building.
5. FSA reinforcements arrive from Limerick.
6. Anti-Treaty forces fall back to Kilmallock.

0 10 20 30 40 50   100   150
metres

Arranged by Shane Walsh

Chapter 3

Fighting for Bruree

The Free State command was keenly aware that Bruree would have to be captured before they could mount a successful push against Kilmallock. The fight for Bruree encompassed some of the fiercest fighting of the battle for Kilmallock. Mainchín Seoighe recalled how, at two years of age, he became a 'war refugee' at this time:

> An IRA man, realising that our locality was likely to become a battle ground, called to our house at Tankardstown, and advised my parents to move to a safer place. And so my parents, my year old sister, and myself, left our home … We were away from home for about a fortnight, during which time fierce fighting took place in the immediate vicinity of our house. And the house bore all the signs of it; windows shattered by bullets, bullet marks on the walls and rafters, and, in one of the fields, a calf killed by gunfire.[1]

The National Army plan was that Major General W. R. E. Murphy would lead the main attack on Bruree from the north-east, using armoured cars in combination with the artillery which had won the day in Limerick city, while Commandant Tom Flood, with his unit of the Dublin Guard, would make a surprise assault from the south-east, via Ballygibba Cross. The eastern approach to Bruree was designed to block anti-Treaty reinforcements from Kilmallock. A series of diversionary and holding operations were launched at Bulgaden, east of Kilmallock, to tie down Republican forces that would otherwise have been available to contribute directly to the defence of Bruree or could have threatened the National Army from the rear.

Four National Army troops were killed in the Ballygibba/ Tankardstown area in the late afternoon of Friday 28 July. Mainchín Seoighe pinpointed the location as a roadside field about 400 yards to the Bruree side of Ballygibba Cross, between Bruree and Kilmallock. The IRA report stated simply that 'a party of enemy troops came in contact with our forces. Four killed and the rest surrendered. Thirteen rifles and one Lewis gun captured by our forces. The enemy failed to break through our lines.'[2] The *Limerick Chronicle* of 1 August carried a report from the special correspondent of the *Irish Independent* on what he had seen in east Limerick over the preceding days:

In Bruff today [30 July] I learned that the bodies of four dead National soldiers had been found last night in a field near Bruree. Their names are – Capt Power, address believed to be Mill Road, Youghal; Pte Patrick [Timothy] Murphy, Pte P. [Patrick] Carey, Inch, Youghal, and Pte D. [Daniel] O'Mahony, Aghada, Co. Cork. All belong to Cork No. 1 Brigade. I inspected the bodies, which lay in the barracks [in Bruff] and found that Capt Power's brains had been blown out and his arms were tied in front about the wrists with what appeared to be a cycle strap. Murphy was shot through the heart, and his boots and leggings are missing. Carey had a terrible wound in the mouth and an injury to his hands, which were coated with dried blood, and O'Mahony was killed by a bullet in the head. The badges were missing from all the caps. As in the case of the three soldiers found dead at Ballingaddy on Monday night last, there was no evidence to show how they met their death. None of their comrades saw them in action, and it is a remarkable thing that all should be hit in such vital parts of the body.

Another account referred to in the *Chronicle* commented further on the case of Captain Power:

It has been erroneously reported that the hands of Capt. Power were tied together when found. That is not so. Dr Higgins tied the hands together so that the body might be placed with ease in a car.

Despite the comparable incident at Ballingaddy earlier that week, it was not common for multiple fatalities to be inflicted in these types of clashes. And the pattern of the fatal wounds – two head wounds, a mouth wound and a heart wound – was extraordinary. But none of the retrospective army accounts of the incident allege an atrocity. The propaganda efforts to arouse suspicions of odious deeds did not prompt retaliation by Provisional Government troops. If these incidents had occurred at a later stage of the war, however, when the Free State was resorting frequently to the mechanisms of terror, the aftermath might have been very different.

Eoin Neeson was the first historian, in 1966, to write a general survey history of the Irish Civil War, and many of his successors have naturally taken their lead from him. It may be the case, however, that this has led to the perpetuation of original errors. Neeson, Calton Younger and many more recent and more localised studies date the conclusive Free State takeover of Bruff (as well as the Free State attack on Bruree which resulted in its capture) to Sunday 30 July. Bruff had been retaken before this, however, and the clash at Ballygibba on Friday 28 July, in which Power, Murphy, Carey and O'Mahony were killed, most likely formed a part of the National Army's main assault on Bruree, albeit a peripheral one, rather than an isolated test of the Republican lines around Kilmallock. *Sgéal Chatha Luimnighe* of 28 July and the *Limerick Chronicle* of 29 July declared that 'Bruree has fallen into the hands of the National Army':

> The garrison, with a large quantity of arms and ammunition, including a Lewis gun, was captured. Some of the irregulars fled on the approach of the National forces, who received a tumultuous welcome as they entered the town. The capture of Bruree renders the position of the irregulars untenable and it is believed that it is only a matter of days until a Kilmallock victory is added to the many others already to the credit of the National forces. The engagement opened with a shock attack by the Dublin Guards (one of the crack units in the army) who were led by Comdt Tom Flood, whose brother, Frank Flood,

was hanged during the war with England. In a very brief space the column of National troops had converged upon the town, which is now liberated from the tyranny of the gunmen.[3]

The *Chronicle* provided additional detail:

Three columns of troops converged on Bruree following a sharp attack by the Dublin Guards. They were supported by heavy artillery but it was only necessary to fire two shells. Some of the irregulars retreated, it is understood, to Kilmallock, leaving a small party in the town and garrison to fight a rearguard action. The latter surrendered almost immediately on the advance party of the National troops reaching the village. When the troops entered the town the people turned out and welcomed them. One publican provided liquid refreshment for any of the troops that came his way and refused to take anything for payment stating that the Irregulars who had occupied the village were worse than the Black and Tans.[4]

Sgéal Chatha Luimnighe usually appeared late in the day and could have covered very recent developments. While the paper, which, it must be remembered, was essentially a propaganda sheet, was not always to be trusted, a famous statement from Eoin O'Duffy, which is widely quoted by historians, seems to confirm the report.

O'Duffy pronounced himself 'well pleased with the progress made by the troops in this command':

We have now cleared East and Mid-Limerick from the Maigue

river to the Tipperary border, and today we have occupied: Castleconnell, Cappamore, Pallas, Oola, Emly, Knocklong – an important line from the Shannon to the Cork border on the East. On the West we occupied Croom yesterday, and today Bruree, holding the Maigue river from the Shannon to near Charleville, I consider the capture of Bruree of much strategic value, making Kilmallock untenable. Kilmallock is now covered on three sides by our troops, and its fall is, I believe, inevitable. The irregulars have also cleared from Athlacca and we occupy Bruff and Rockbarton.

This statement was published in both *Sgéal Chatha Luim-nighe* and *The Freeman's Journal* on Monday 31 July, but it had appeared in the *Limerick Chronicle* on Saturday 29 July, having been issued by the publicity department of the South Western Command on 28 July. This department was responsible for *Sgéal Chatha Luimnighe*, of course, but the timing of O'Duffy's statement certainly disrupts the consensus on the chronology of events. It might well be simply pre-emptive propaganda, however, predicting the fall of Bruff rather than relaying news that it had actually happened. The *Chronicle* of 1 August, for instance, mentioned that 'It is reported … that the Irregulars are retreating from Kilmallock.' In this case, the paper was four days ahead of events. However, the details of the assault on Bruree included in *Sgéal Chatha Luimnighe* and the *Chronicle* on 28 and 29 July were accurate and in line with what was reported in the following days when more information became available. Michael Hopkinson's *Green against Green*, which is the most authoritative account of the history of the Civil War, does not enumerate a specific date in regard to the Free State victories in Bruff and Bruree. Hopkinson, however, does refer to a three-day period between the Free State victory and the Republican counter-attack in Bruff, which conforms to the traditional sequence of 30 July–2 August. The questioning of existing accounts here is open to correction or contradiction. Michael Harrington, for instance, does seem to be on firm ground when he sets 30 July as the date of the Bruree attack. He cites a Republican communiqué which describes how:

> … at 7.30 p.m. last night an advance was made on Bruree by Free State forces numbering approx. 300 being supported by three armoured cars and several machine-guns. A small section of our men numbering about twelve were occupying Bruree and railway bridge convenient. Due to Lewis gun fire they found it impossible to hold the bridge and had to with-draw. Scouts at Clogheen Hill had been surrounded and taken prisoner. Lost twelve men, eleven rifles and one Lewis gun.[5]

The tactical consequences of the defeat were readily acknow-ledged by the Republican leadership and the loss of Bruree was referred to as a 'catastrophe'. It appears, based on Harrington's interpretation, that this source clearly identifies the date of the attack as 30 July. John Pinkman's diaries indicate likewise: on 29 July his unit marched to Bruff, which they found to be 'safely in the hands of our own forces'. They spent that night billeted in some of the houses in Bruff before setting out the following morning for Bruree. It should be pointed out here, however, that the minutiae of Pinkman's memoirs are occasionally, if understandably, inexact, especially in regard to time. Pinkman was part of an advance party of about fifteen which proceeded before the rest of the column and on a different route. They came under fire two miles outside Bruree and were delayed. By the time they reached Bruree, the Republicans had already departed. The main body of the company had already arrived but they had run into 'fierce opposition' at the railway bridge and had to send back to Bruff for the eighteen-pounder field gun, which was returned to Bruff once it had performed its duty and dislodged the anti-Treatyites.[6]

The Republican bulletin in *The Cork Examiner* of 31 July included much the same detail as the internal IRA document quoted by Harrington, apart from its reference to two rather than three armoured cars. Unfortunately, parts of the bulletin are no longer legible. Those sections which are did not mention a specific date. What *The Cork Examiner* did say, however, was that:

> Simultaneous with this attack [on Bruree] an advance was attempted by the enemy on the Republican lines all along east to Bulgaden. At Ballygubba [Ballygibba] Cross a party of 16 Free State troops came in contact with the Republican forces, who immediately opened fire on them with the result that four of the Free State party were killed and the remainder surrendered. Twelve prisoners, 15 rifles, 1 Lewis gun, revolvers and ammunition, were captured by our forces in this encounter. The enemy failed to break through our lines.[7]

This incident took place on 28 July and it is significant that the

Republican-controlled *Cork Examiner* has timed it as happening simultaneously with the Free State capture of Bruree. Karl Murphy also puts the Ballygibba Cross incident and the Bruree attack together.[8] This suggests that there was more to O'Duffy's 28 July declaration of victory in Bruree than wishful thinking.

Again, the purpose of this argument is simply to raise questions of chronology which do not seem to have been fully and satisfactorily answered heretofore due to conflicting sources. The contention here, then, is that the final Free State victory in Bruree occurred on 28 July rather than 30 July as has generally been assumed by historians before now. This must lead to a revision of our understanding of how the last week of the battle for Kilmallock unfolded.

Both W. R. E. Murphy and Tom Flood used Bruff as the launching pad for their attacks on Bruree, which was an important position in its own right, surrounded by hillocks and flanked on the east by the Croom–Charleville railway and on the west by the River Maigue. The weather had improved considerably since the previous week and was no longer a hindrance to large-scale troop or convoy movements. The National Army soldiers were accompanied by commandeered cars and charabancs. The armoured car 'Danny Boy' was also present. Murphy's column was delayed at Dromin due to a demolished bridge, but they filled in the gap and continued, also having to remove felled trees from the road. The two-sided operation proved successful.

The Republican defenders were surprised and caught in Free State crossfire. The anti-Treatyites withdrew only after five hours of dogged resistance. The last IRA cover party, a dozen of whom were captured, had held the railway bridge until artillery fire, in combination with Lewis gun fire, made their position unsustainable and the National Army seized the town. Bruree lies in a depression surrounded by hillocks and would have been particularly vulnerable to artillery. The pro-Treaty victory may have been delayed by the fact that their artillery gunners were prevented from firing for a time by a herd of cattle, which may also have facilitated the IRA disengagement.[9] In any case, once again it was the artillery which decided this battle.

O'Duffy may have believed that the fall of Kilmallock was now 'inevitable', but the Republicans were not so accepting of this fate. They were unwilling to leave Kilmallock completely vulnerable to attack from both Bruff and Bruree, and made efforts to redress their strategic deficit. By temporarily holding Patrickswell and attempting to recapture Bruff they hoped to reassert their regional superiority, in the process buttressing Kilmallock. Lack of manpower and, in some instances, appropriate firepower, limited the effectiveness of this plan, but it was ultimately scuppered when the National Army used the sea to land significant numbers of their troops on the Kerry coast, behind the anti-Treatyite defensive line.

On the night of Monday 31 July anti-Treatyites moved against the rectory on the outskirts of Kilmallock, which was garrisoned by twelve Provisional Government troops. Both the *Limerick Chronicle* and *Sgéal Chatha Luimnighe*, but not *The Freeman's Journal* which also carried an account of the incident, alleged that the Free Staters were subjected to further attack after they had surrendered:

They had come out of the building, leaving their arms behind, and were standing outside when a bomb was thrown at them. Three of the troops were wounded, and the remainder, taking the incident as a forewarning of what their treatment might be when prisoners, decided to effect an escape. The troops succeeded in getting away, and have reported back to their unit.[10]

A second IRA unit, equipped with an armoured car, a Lewis gun, a Maxim gun and a Thompson gun, attacked another house which had been occupied by Free State forces. They took eight prisoners and added twelve rifles, one Lewis gun, ammunition and rifle grenades to their already impressive arsenal.[11] These two actions may well have been led by West Cork columns, commanded respectively by Maurice Donegan and Dan Holland.[12] They were only minor successes, however, and relatively meaningless when compared with the Free State victory in Tipperary town on 1 August. Apart from the capture of Limerick and Waterford, Eoin Neeson judged the capture of Tipperary as the most significant operation yet against the anti-Treaty line. Besides isolating Clonmel, it broadened the front against Cork and opened the Kilmallock flank.[13]

Meanwhile, the Republican forces in County Limerick focused their energies on Patrickswell, which they captured at 2 a.m. on 2 August. Patrickswell was most tactically useful in respect of Bruree and the objective was to mount a Republican counter-attack on that town, which began only a few hours later. The purpose of occupying Patrickswell was to pre-empt enemy intervention from the north at Bruree, which would take the shape of reinforcements from Limerick city.

According to IRA Volunteer Peter Hogan, A Company, 2nd Battalion, Mid Limerick Brigade, it was Henry Meaney who gave the order to attack Patrickswell, and he was subsequently killed in action. Some twenty-five Free State prisoners were taken, along with quantities of rifles and ammunition.[14] A detachment of the National Army under Brigadier Michael Keane succeeded in effecting the release of five of the prisoners. The Republican occupation of Patrickswell lasted less than twenty-four hours. They withdrew westwards when the IRA counter-attack on Bruree failed and large contingents of pro-Treaty troops started to move from Limerick city towards the Kerry border. A unit of the Dublin Guard under Tom Keogh and Jimmy Slattery, who was also a former member of Michael Collins' Squad, reclaimed Patrickswell for the Free State. This is a good example of the effectiveness of the Provisional Government's policy of using small groups of Dublin Guards to bolster the untried troops who formed a significant proportion of the National Army. The *Limerick Chronicle* described one of the engagements that had occurred in the town:

> The troops at once dismounted and approached the barricade cautiously but found no one there. The road here appeared to be mined, but on closer examination it was found that this piece of work was mere camouflage. The troops cautiously pushed on, and proceeded but about 100 yards on foot when terrific fire was opened on them from both sides of the road and near the village. The troops replied, and for some minutes the fire was intense. The officer in charge of the troops concluded that he was opposed to a much superior force … He effected a

gallant rearguard action, with one slight casualty. The irregulars attempted to surround the small convoy, but a skilful flanking movement defeated this object. The advance party of the troops states that they were fired at from houses on both sides of the road, and also from the railway embankment. When the first volley was fired three men were noticed near one of the houses, one of whom was in uniform. They raised their hands, and then dashed into the house. As they disappeared a volley was sent through the door after them, with what result is unknown. It cannot be stated with any certainty whether Henry Meaney was shot in this encounter or an earlier one.[15]

Meaney, from John Street, was a prominent and popular figure in Limerick city and the news of his death was greeted with regret. He had been a long-term member of the Volunteer movement (including the Redmondite National Volunteers for a time) and was imprisoned for political offences on a number of occasions. He had served as president of the Limerick Branch of the Irish Transport and General Workers' Union, and was also a member of the Munster Council of the Gaelic Athletic Association. He was buried in the Republican plot in Mount St Lawrence.[16] When the Limerick branch of the Irish Transport and General Workers' Union next met it extended its sympathy to Meaney's family. When Limerick Corporation met on Thursday night, 3 August, the meeting was adjourned as a tribute of respect to the memory of the fallen in the city and country generally. Councillor M. Reddan had proposed adjournment as a sign of respect to Henry Meaney and Harry Boland specifically.[17]

George Tighe from Patrickswell was twelve or thirteen during the fighting there. In 1933 he wrote an article on the events of 2 August 1922 based on his diary entries from the time. It gives a clear indication of the type of disruption suffered by civilians. Tighe's family home was one of a number in the village which had been occupied by National Army troops, many of whom were apparently drunk. The house came under fire during the Republican attack and one of the Free State soldiers was seriously wounded. They surrendered when the Republicans took a sledgehammer to the door and threatened to bomb the house. Tighe was then sent to fetch the local doctor for the injured party. On his way back he was caught in the middle of another exchange. When he eventually reached home he found that:

> All the windows in our house had been shattered, and the walls and roof also had received considerable damage. We later discovered that money and other property had been taken by one or other of the parties.[18]

After 2 a.m. on 2 August, when Patrickswell was taken over by Republicans, the way was clear for the anti-Treatyites in Kilmallock to counter-attack Bruree. Tom Flood was the Free State commander in Bruree. He had his HQ in the Railway Hotel, which covered the bridge and the main road from Kilmallock. There were other pro-Treaty strong points at Bruree Lodge, a large country house on the Charleville road, and in the schoolhouse on the Newcastlewest road. (John Pinkman, who was one of the Free State defenders of Bruree, suggested that Flood based himself and his HQ in Bruree Lodge and that Captain Jackie Byrne from Tipperary was in charge of the Railway Hotel, but this does not seem to have been the case.)

The counter-attack started at 6.30 a.m. The Republican force, equipped with the only trench mortar in the IRA, nicknamed 'Lizzie', and accompanied by at least two and possibly three improvised armoured cars fitted with Lewis and Thompson guns, left Ash Hill Towers for Bruree in two columns. The National Army report on the engagement estimated the number of anti-Treaty fighters at 500, which was certainly an exaggeration. The Republicans made the most progress at the schoolhouse position, which was under Captain Dinan. A sentry was posted to guard a bridge leading up to the schoolhouse. When a Republican armoured car approached the bridge the sentry assumed it was friendly and was captured. The armoured car then proceeded to ram the door of the school and to put a machine gun through one of its windows. About two hours into the counter-attack the Republicans took fifteen prisoners at the school outpost.

The IRA also made a concerted effort to seize Bruree Lodge, using machine guns and rifle grenades. Pinkman was stationed in the Lodge:

We expected the brunt of the attack would be launched on the front of the house and we immediately barricaded the doors with as much furniture as we could find. Our big Lewis gunner mounted his machine gun behind the barricades in case the attackers tried to burst in through the front entrance.

The attackers closed in on the house and we realised we were surrounded, cut off from any possible escape. At first,

Irregular snipers tried to pick us off by firing through the windows. Then they fired grenades at the house. But it wasn't until we were attacked by mortar bombs that we became really worried. We never suspected that the Irregulars possessed a mortar until the shells began to land around us. Fortunately we were able to hold off the Irregulars so that they weren't able to get close enough to land any direct hits on the building, but the grounds in front of the house became pock-marked with crater holes. If the Irregulars had been able to get us within range of their grenade and mortar fire we would have been finished. There was little else we could do but accept the fact that we were under siege, hold out as long as we were able and hope that relief would come from the main force of National Army troops coming from Kilmallock. We were running short of ammunition and had to ration our dwindling supply of food.

In mid-afternoon on the second day of the siege [this is an example of Pinkman's erroneous timing – the counter-attack lasted several hours rather than two days], the firing from the Irregulars gradually died down and we thought they were withdrawing at the approach of a column sent to relieve us. After the firing had ceased for a while, most of us were glad of the opportunity to venture outside for fresh air and a chance to stretch our legs … All of a sudden the sound of rifle fire broke out [Pinkman was pinned down outside without his rifle but managed to get back safely to the house] …

Our worst moments came on the final day of the siege when the Irregulars drove an improvised armoured car to within six feet of the front door of the lodge. During a furious exchange of fire, the rear doors of the armoured vehicle flew open and some of its occupants made a reckless attempt to storm the lodge. The intensity of our firing drove all of them back to the vehicle except one who was left badly injured on the ground. When a comrade returned to pick him up one of our lads cried, 'An act of mercy!' and we all ceased firing until the wounded man was back inside the armoured car.

We then expected the vehicle to retire completely from the fray but were surprised to see it halt only a short distance from the lodge and return for two more desperate assaults. But the vehicle was being driven in such an increasingly erratic manner that we concentrated our fire on its more vulnerable parts – including the gaps in its armoured plating – in an effort to disable it totally. I don't know if we did more injury to the car than to its crew, but after the third assault the vehicle lumbered off and then careened wildly down the road and out of sight.

When our supplies of food and ammunition were getting so low that we couldn't have held out much longer, the Irregulars stopped their attack.[19]

The IRA counter-attack made least headway against Tom Flood's command. The Republicans utilised their second armoured car here but continued to concentrate their fire on the Railway Hotel while Flood moved his men, under the cover of a Lewis gunner, to a more secure adjacent building. The anti-Treatyites withdrew from Bruree altogether as Free State reinforcements under General Séamas Hogan and General Galvin arrived from Limerick with the Whippet (an armoured car) known as 'The Customs House'. Patrickswell was also abandoned at this stage. Hogan personally led the relief force to Bruree, reportedly travelling in the single turreted Rolls Royce armoured car. 'The Customs House', according to *Sgéal Chatha Luimnighe* and the *Limerick Chronicle*, proceeded to pursue the two Republican armoured cars to within a mile of Kilmallock.[20] The third Republican armoured car, which happened to be 'The River Lee', had seemingly developed engine trouble *en route* and it apparently followed 'The Customs House' into Bruree. Realising that the town was still in Free State hands, 'The River Lee' fled down the road to Kilmallock after its two companions, with Hogan in hot pursuit. A confrontation that supposedly ensued between 'The Customs House' and the three Republican armoured cars was cut short because the Vickers machine gun in the Free State vehicle jammed and forced Hogan to break off the engagement.[21] This sequence of fighting around Bruree is a prime example of how some operations were designed to capitalise on the speed and power of armoured vehicles rather than to rely solely on infantry.

With the exception of Kilmallock, pro-Treaty dominance of all of south and east Limerick was now assured. Only in the Castleconnell/Newport area outside Limerick city and near the Tipperary border, where Seán Carroll and Paddy Ryan (Lacken) remained highly active, was there prolonged significant Republican activity. There were other isolated pockets of resistance, however. In late August, for instance, W. R. E. Murphy had to move against a forty-strong Republican column that had occupied Glenstal Castle near Murroe. He planned that on 24

August four columns would approach the castle from the north, south, east and west. Murphy would lead the southern force from Limerick consisting of seventy-eight men and 'The Customs House' along with two Lancias. The castle had been evacuated by the time the Free State forces arrived but 7,000 rounds of ammunition and a Lewis gun had apparently been left behind.[77]

The failure of the Bruree counter-attack had significant consequences for the morale of both sides and it effectively ended any further Republican offensive in the area. The Republican mainstay of Kilmallock was now badly exposed. The National Army held a semi-circular line around the town from Bruree in the west, past the village of Dromin in the north, through Bulgaden and on to Riversfield House in the south-east. All was now in place for the Free State attack on Kilmallock to proceed.

CHAPTER 4

THE BATTLE FOR KILMALLOCK

Sgéal Chatha Luimnighe declared Kilmallock and its inhabitants to be 'in a state of siege' during the last week of July, with people 'confined to their homes', but expecting that the National Army would soon relieve the burden:

> Very few people are allowed to leave and that only when they are able to satisfy the irregular sentries as to their bona-fides. Still fewer [are] permitted to enter, for having passed the National outposts, who are stationed in the district, one has also to give satisfactory answers to queries by the irregulars. No business whatever is being transacted and people are remaining indoors, not knowing the moment at which hostilities may break out. The irregulars have seized large quantities of food and provisions, and the poor are feeling it hard to procure the necessities of life. Trees are felled on all the roads and barricades erected. Squads of snipers were placed in positions dominating the various entrances. On the right of the road between Bruff and Kilmallock, on the main road, is Kilmallock Hill, from which snipers are operating. ... The National forces now completely dominate the town and

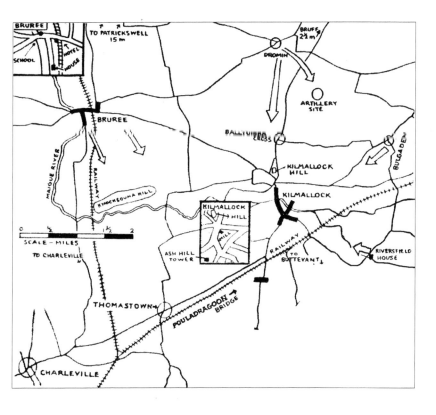

since the victories at Bruff and Bruree there seems to be little hope for the irregulars there.[1]

The only fighting in the vicinity of the town at this stage was restricted to sniping. *The New York Times* of 1 August reported that 'people continue to leave the town'. The same edition of the paper, however, based on a wireless message from Limerick on 31 July, stated that 'The national posts in the Kilmallock area have been pushed close to the town but except for sniping no engagement has developed.' The Provisional Government positions in the area, such as the one in the rectory, had actually been pushed back on 31 July.

The New York Times was more accurate in its overall analysis of the situation:

> ... the irregulars have been busily strengthening their defences. Estimates of the number of mutineers in and around Kilmallock vary from 200 to 500. Their commander seems to be a man of more than average military capacity, to judge from the dispositions he has made of his forces. So far as can be detected good use has been made of the heights dominating the town for the placing of concealed posts.

National Army Operation Order No. 6 was drawn up by General W. R. E. Murphy. It detailed how the pro-Treatyites proposed to take Kilmallock and outlined the sequence of advances by the various bodies of troops which would lead to the capture of the town. Murphy's plans were, however, hampered somewhat by the lack of basic military training within the ranks of the National Army. Karl Murphy contends that the attack had to be postponed three times because officers failed to prepare their men in a punctual fashion. In fact, he suggests that a whole day was lost because a quartermaster failed to feed the troops appropriately. Furthermore, many of the officers were inexperienced in following sophisticated operational instructions: 'we had never seen the likes of them' recalled Jackie Byrne. There was bewilderment at General Murphy's order that trenches should be dug, and this is often seen as evidence that his military philosophy was hopelessly conditioned by his experiences in the First World War, which were not immediately relevant in this setting. The order applied only to Knocksouna Hill, however, and it did help to prevent casualties among the Free State forces there when they came under machine-gun fire later in the day.[2]

Operation Order No. 6 was circulated to all relevant officers, i.e. those commanding units involved in the assault, at 3 p.m. on 3 August.[3] The attack was set to begin at 6 a.m. on 4 August and the operation would involve the whole front line from Adare to Kilmallock. Murphy was to establish his advance HQ at Ballycullane, on the northern outskirts of Kilmallock. Colonel Commandant Tom Keogh, with his column of the Dublin Guard, was to attack Adare at 6 a.m. from the east. Michael Keane, with his men of the West Limerick Brigade, was to simultaneously attack Adare from the south.

A garrison of twenty-five men would remain in Bruree and act as a flank guard while Commandant Tom Flood would attempt to establish an entrenched position on Knocksouna Hill with the rest of his unit, numbering ninety-six. From here it was expected that Flood would be able to contain any Republican retreat in the direction of Charleville. Flood's left flank would be covered by a detachment of sixty members of the Limerick City Brigade under Captain Casey, who would extend the attack in the direction of Tankardstown.

One hundred and thirty-eight 1st Dublin Brigade Regulars under Captain Dominick were charged with capturing Dalton's Hill, from where they would advance on the west side of Kil-mallock and take control of Ash Hill Towers. Dominick would have some assistance from General Galvin, commanding 366 men of the 1st Southern Division. One hundred of these men would initially be positioned at the Forge Cross at Ballymuddagh. From there they were to attack Ballygibba at 6 a.m. They would approach from the east and concentrate on the left flank. Galvin was then expected to clear Grange Hill of the enemy. For this task he would have 120 men at his disposal. When Grange Hill was successfully cleared, according to Murphy, 'this will clear Kilmallock and form line on S.W. of the town'. At this stage, Galvin, using fifty men, was to attack westwards along the railway and act in unison with Dominick's force attacking Ash Hill Towers.

Donnchadh O'Hannigan and Colonel Scannell were to hold a reserve force of 100 East Limerick men at the crossroads south of Greenpark House. 'The pursuit,' stressed Murphy, 'must be rapid and unceasing.' The decisive advantage enjoyed by the Free State army, of course, was the 18-pounder artillery piece which would be in position two miles north of Kilmallock by 5.45 a.m. It would first support the infantry attacks on Grange Hill and Dalton's Hill before ranging on Ash Hill Towers.[4] The Whippet armoured car 'Danny Boy', equipped with a Vickers machine gun, would also be called into action as appropriate and operations would be coordinated from Murphy's HQ at Ballycullane. The general used 'Danny Boy' as a reconnaissance vehicle during the attack. He had a lucky escape at one point when the engine stalled for some minutes within sight of a Republican machine-gun post.[5]

Eoin O'Duffy's initial assurance after the fall of Bruree that the Republican hold on Kilmallock was now 'untenable' and its fall to the National Army 'inevitable' (see p. 92) may have wavered somewhat in the days following. Republican resistance around Bruff, and IRA initiatives at Patrickswell and Bruree suggested that there was plenty of fight left in them.

Perhaps more worrying from the Free State perspective were intelligence reports on 4 August that there were as many as 1,000 anti-Treatyites within one mile south and west of Kilmallock. The daily report of the South Western Command put 600 of these men in Kilmallock itself and 400 between Kilmallock and Charleville. Railway links with Buttevant and Mitchelstown were good. There was a flying column of seventy men based in Tully and another of fifty based in Ardpatrick. All these areas offered close support to Kilmallock. Republican forces were not only numerous but well-armed with rifles, machine guns and the necessary ammunition, as well as rifle grenades, 'one or two armoured lorries and a plentiful supply of explosives and mines ... with about twenty lorries used as transport for men and material'.[6]

Despite the concern caused by these reports, however, Operation Order No. 6 went ahead as planned. If the pro-Treaty estimations of the strength of anti-Treaty forces in the area are accurate, then Republicans initially had approximately 400 more men available for the defence of Kilmallock than the Free State had on hand for the attack. In this context, the significance of the availability of artillery becomes readily apparent. In addition to an eighteen-pounder field gun, the pro-Treaty forces massing at Kilmallock were boosted by the timely arrival of 700 reinforcements from Limerick.[7] Among the Free State troops who fought in the Bruff-Bruree-Kilmallock triangle were 250 men under Brigadier Tom O'Connor Scarteen, many of them new recruits from east Kerry and the Cobh and Youghal areas of Cork. O'Connor Scarteen was the only significant Kerry War of Independence commander to go pro-Treaty. Along with the new recruits, his unit included some veterans of the Northern Division, as well as a brother of a Provisional Government minister, Kevin O'Higgins.[8]

The plan of attack emphasised the importance of the four hills surrounding and overlooking Kilmallock. Knocksouna Hill, two miles to the west and overlooking the Loobagh river and the road to Charleville, was recognised as being important, but Ash Hill to the south-west, Kilmallock Hill directly to the north and Quarry Hill to the north-east were prioritised, as they dominated the town. The aim of the initial wave of the assault was to capture these hills, after which the troops would 'push forward to Ballygubba [Ballygibba] Cross from Forge Cross, establishing a straight line from Kilmallock to Knocksouna'. The attack, originally scheduled to start at 6 a.m., was delayed for more than two hours because the artillery unit had not reconnoitred their assigned positions.[9]

The commander of the artillery section was General Mc-Cormick.[10] The guns were trained on Kilmallock Hill from a hill outside the village of Dromin, about three and a half miles from Kilmallock.[11] The troops were *in situ* from 6.30 a.m. and the firing of the first shell at 8.30 a.m. signalled the beginning of the attack. The target was a house belonging to a family named Strafford which was located immediately in front of the 1st Southern Division's assembly point and thought to be a Republican machine-gun post. Another such machine-gun post, at the house of a family named Walsh, was also shelled. The infantry then advanced. The 1st Southern came under Thompson machine-gun and rifle fire but did not sustain any casualties. The 1st Dublin Brigade Regulars made rapid progress until they encountered stiff resistance and heavy fire from Thompson machine guns and rifles on the slopes of Kilmallock Hill, which slowed them considerably. Free State forces adapted quickly and improvised to an extent:

> Captain Dominick then extended his flank to the east and advanced on the hill from two directions, east and north. The armoured car was then brought into action, and the artillery brought to bear on the Irregulars in the quarries. Fox's Mount, a house on the hill, was then taken and half the hill was in our hands. Five casualties were sustained, all slightly wounded.[12]

The account of the fighting in *The New York Times* also pointed to the role of the artillery in breaking Republican resistance here:

> Had it not been for the timely assistance of the guns it is likely the troops would still be held up before Kilmallock Hill, from which they could advance no further because of the enemy's deadly machine gun and rifle fire. Shells from the guns blotted out the trenches and the infantry swept on to join up with other units on Quarry Hill.[13]

Progress had been less pronounced in the early stages of the attack on Quarry Hill: 'The officers of the 1st Southern did not grip their men and push them on from position to position.

This was done for them and their unit brought up into line.'
The East Limerick Brigade detachment under Colonel Scannell
had to fill a gap between the 1st Southern and Dublin Regulars.
The artillery then shelled quarries where Republicans had based
themselves and quickly dislodged the defenders. At 12.30 p.m.
the lines re-formed at the foot of the Quarry and Kilmallock
Hills. A general advance was now ordered:

> A heavy burst of fire was opened on the Irregulars from cottages
> on Kilmallock Hill, and a barricade of a steamroller with a mine
> in front was encountered. While pulling the wires out of the
> mine a concentrated burst of fire swept the party engaged in
> this work, but no casualties resulted. The barricade was removed
> and the armoured car advanced followed closely by the infantry.
> The crest of the hill was thus cleared. Sniping and Thompson
> fire still came from a cluster of houses on the main Bruff–
> Kilmallock road. The 18-pounder silenced this fire and our
> infantry occupied the position.

Flood's Dublin Guard had little trouble occupying Knocksouna Hill.

Meanwhile, at Ballygibba the pro-Treaty forces had engaged
the Republicans from the east and captured the relevant positions after an hour of fighting. A detachment of the Limerick
City Brigade garrisoned Bruree during the advance on Kilmallock. The Free State army had established dominance of all the
heights overlooking the town by 3.30 p.m. A sniping contest
ensued while the pro-Treaty troops consolidated these newly
won positions. At this stage 'it was decided that, owing to the

fatigue of the men, the task of clearing the remainder of the town would be postponed till morning'.[14] They had been on the move almost constantly for a number of days.

Free State forces were now within half a mile of the town centre.[15] The experience of Bruree being still fresh in pro-Treaty minds, they wanted to consolidate the lines against any potential counter-attack and for much of the night 'the National encampment was assailed on all sides by roving bands of Irregulars who made surprise sorties'. These Republican units 'put up a stiff fight' and 'kept up an intermittent fire until close on dawn'.[16]

There was nothing of substance that might be regarded as a counter-attack, however, and 'the task of clearing the remainder of the town' proved much easier than might have been anticipated:

> On 5/8/22 at 5.30 a.m. Kilmallock was entered by our troops. Eight prisoners (four with arms), an ambulance and a quantity of ammunition were captured. Mines were removed and roads cleared. All bridges, buildings etc. were intact. An outpost line from Kilmallock westwards along Tankardstown and Knock-souna ridges was established.[17]

'This most redoubtable fortress,' according to *The New York Times*, 'was vacated at 8 o'clock last night [4 August] and from midnight onwards bands of beaten mutineers, numbering hundreds, began to quit the town.'[18] The publicity department of the National Army elaborated on, and exaggerated, the circumstances of the entry of the Free State troops into Kilmallock:

When the troops arrived in the Town they received a tumultu-
ous reception by the inhabitants, who expressed their sincere
delight to be rid of the irregulars, whom they described as
'worse than the black and tans'. The Town – including Railway
Station and all Bridges – is practically intact – the mines
having been removed by the troops. Ashill [*sic*] Towers is also
occupied. During the fight for the Town the irregulars seized
eight civilians and forced them to build barricades under the
fire of the Troops. The civilians strongly protested and the
irregulars threatened to blow their brains out if they did not
do the work. Eight prisoners were taken with a quantity of
rifles and ammunition. The casualties amongst the troops were
slight. The Officer in charge of the town has issued an order:
1 – To close all public houses. 2 – To restore all looted property
to Ashill Towers. 3 – To open all shops.[19]

According to the *Limerick Chronicle*, the locals gave the arriving
troops 'a tremendous ovation. Some officers who were known
in the locality, were embarrassed by women-folk, who were
overjoyed at the relief of the town.'[20]

Fr John Carr of Glenfield told Mainchín Seoighe how he
remembered, as a boy, 'seeing the town crowded with soldiers':

Many of the exhausted troops were lying on the sidewalks,
sound asleep, their guns beside them. Next day, Sunday, the
church was packed with soldiers attending the 11 o'clock
Mass, and as the congregation were leaving the church at the
end of Mass, Pa MacCarthy played 'The Soldier's Song' on the
organ.[21]

Another observer in Kilmallock during late July and early August was Dr William Turner, Bishop of Buffalo. Turner was on a visit to his family, who resided near Kilmallock, where he himself was born in 1871.[22] On 7 August he preached about his experience in Kilmallock to the Arch-Confraternity of the Holy Family in the Church of St Alphonsus in Limerick city. He had little to say that was complimentary:

> … they in America … never imagined they should come back to this country to find Irishmen fighting amongst themselves. The Bishop, proceeding, reminded his congregation that he was expected to be present at the celebrations on Sunday in connection with the Feast of St Alphonsus. The reason he could not be present … he was in Kilmallock and could not reach the city. While his lordship was in Kilmallock he learned a good deal by personal observation in regard to the destruction of property, especially the looting of the workhouse of Kilmallock, including the residence of the Nuns … Neither the sacred character of the Nuns nor their work for suffering humanity was considered by the crowds from the back lanes of Kilmallock nor were they protected by the so-called Irish Republicans during the two whole weeks that they continued to load their carts and wagons with what was after all the property of the people. Only a third of the destruction was done by fire, and from his lordship's own personal observation, he realised that the main part of the destruction was due to wanton looting.[23]

Operation Order No. 6 had been implemented almost seamlessly. Its various strands had come together efficiently and the

117

targets it set had been met. Kilmallock, one of the major bastions of the Munster Republic, was now under the control of the Provisional Government. The unforgiving verdict of Joseph Curran was that:

> Although it was the longest and hardest-fought battle of the civil war, Kilmallock was more a clash between armed mobs than a conventional engagement between regular armies. Not only were many of the soldiers untrained for combat, very few of the officers could direct more than 100 men in any kind of firefight.[24]

Giving the benefit of the doubt to the National Army, one might say that this victory was the result of General Murphy's brilliant planning, the competence of his officers, and the bravery and fighting ability of their troops in combination with the impact of artillery. However, this would be to ignore the reality that there was no final battle for Kilmallock, no all-out last stand, no 'No Surrender'. The Republicans had chosen to abandon the town.

The majority of anti-Treatyites had apparently withdrawn from the town before the attack was launched and had headed south to Charleville before Flood could position himself to cut them off. The first coastal landings had gone ahead, however, and there would be no need for street fighting in Kilmallock itself. The troops at Riversfield House had remained there in order to cover a possible Republican retreat to Buttevant. The fighting which had occurred, such as on the slopes of Kilmallock Hill, had been conducted as a rearguard delaying action by the Cork IRA brigades to facilitate the retreat of the main body of Republicans from Kilmallock. It was little more than token resistance. 'The experience and dash of the Dublin Guard had contributed much to ultimate success in the long wearing-down process around Kilmallock,' wrote Calton Younger, 'but the main reason for the Republicans allowing their front door to give so easily was the news that intruders had burst in the back.'[25]

The Kerry brigades had evacuated because a contingent of the Dublin Guard led by General Paddy Daly had landed at Fenit in north Kerry, seven miles from Tralee, on 2 August. For the Kerry Republicans in Limerick, as Michael Harrington put it, 'defence of the kingdom of Kerry took precedence over protection of the "Republic of Munster"'.[26]

The Republicans had been outflanked and were thus forced to abandon their linear defensive strategy. Even without the added dimension of the seaborne manoeuvres, however, the overwhelming strength of the almost 2,000 Free State troops converging on Kilmallock, backed up by artillery, would almost certainly have forced a Republican retreat in the short term. Despite the devastating effects of the Free State's field guns in Limerick city and Waterford, the Republican forces around Kilmallock had made no real preparations for defence against artillery. Moreover, no real effort, either before or after the shelling started, was made to disable the eighteen-pounder. This may be a harsh criticism of the Republicans, given that the Free Staters clearly appreciated the value of their artillery and afforded it suitable protection, but it is another illustration of Republican powerlessness.

Younger suggested that the surprise landings gave the National Army 'the dual advantage of meeting little opposition, because of the absence of large numbers of the Kerry fighting men in Kilmallock, and of shortening the struggle for Kilmallock'.[27] This is an accurate assessment, but it is incomplete. A substantial proportion of the Kilmallock garrison was made up of men of the Kerry brigades. Tom Doyle estimated that as many as 250 to 300 of Kerry's most experienced Republican fighters were in the area around the Bruff-Bruree-Kilmallock triangle.[28] Because of Kilmallock, there were little more than a handful of anti-Treaty troops at Fenit and Tralee. The bulk of the Tralee Kerry No. 1 Brigade, commanded by Humphrey Murphy, was engaged at Kilmallock under the command of Vice-Brigadier J. J. Sheehy.[29] Daly did not know this at the time of his landing, however. In fact, according to Doyle, Daly 'had no intelligence on either the strength, disposition or the defences of the Republican forces he would encounter as the troops under his command set foot on Kerry soil'.[30]

This was an appalling risk to take and was indicative of how the Free State often blundered through major operations, their shortcomings not being highlighted simply because the enemy was not strong enough to do so. Eoin O'Duffy, however, to give him his due, had foreseen the potential for disaster. This may have been made easier for him because of his 'acidic relationship' with Dalton.[31] On 26 July O'Duffy advised Richard Mulcahy:

I would consider a landing ... anywhere on the Cork or Kerry coast, unwise for the present. There would be an immediate concentration of Irregulars and our troops would be immediately surrounded. They might make a fight, but I fear that would be all.[32]

From this perspective, the Free Staters would have been happy to detain the Kerry and Cork Republicans in Kilmallock until the landings had taken place. In any case, good fortune probably played as much of a role in the successful landings as good planning.

Nonetheless, in capturing Tralee the pro-Treatyites had gained a foothold behind the anti-Treaty lines. The National Army was about to split what Eoin Neeson referred to as 'the lowland north from the highland south-west' of the remains of the Munster Republic.[33] Simultaneously with the landing at Fenit, Provisional Government troops advanced from Clare and Limerick, and the Free Staters soon controlled north Kerry. South Kerry, more remote and mountainous, proved a much more difficult task, however, and the war dragged on there for several more months. Free State forces were set to land in Cork on 7 August. In response to this development, Liam Lynch informed Ernie O'Malley on 9 August, Republican forces on the Limerick front 'have been reduced, and are forming into columns'.[34] The most active and most efficient Cork and Kerry Republicans had been in Limerick when the sea landings started. They were demoralised and exhausted after Kilmallock.[35] The Republican retreat from Kilmallock may have started out in a controlled and orderly fashion but it soon gathered pace and became 'disorderly' according to Liam Deasy:

Men were constantly arriving at Buttevant Barracks en route to their home areas ... The constant stream of Volunteers retreating from Limerick and Kilmallock were sadly dejected and in a bad mood.[36]

Kilmallock was by no means unique in being a former anti-Treaty stronghold which was now in pro-Treaty hands. By the beginning of August the same had happened in the cities of Waterford, Limerick and Galway, and the towns of Carrick-on-Suir, Tipperary, Castlebar, Ballina, Dundalk, Wexford and Sligo.

CHAPTER 5

FIGHTING FOR
WEST LIMERICK

The speed of events seemed to increase markedly after the fall of
Kilmallock, as if it had opened the floodgates for the Free State
army to pour into the rest of the county. *Sgéal Chatha Luimnighe* published, on a daily basis, lists of towns newly occupied.
On Tuesday 8 August the news from the previous weekend
was that, along with Kilmallock, Listowel, Adare, Rathkeale,
Broadford, Askeaton, Ballingarry, Kilfinny and Kilmacow were
now in Free State hands. On 9 August the newspaper reported
that there had been 'stiff fighting' at Rathkeale, Broadford,
Askeaton and Ballingarry, after which 'the people accorded
the troops a tremendous welcome'. General Eoin O'Duffy and
General Fionán Lynch of the Dublin Guard, who was a TD
for Kerry–West Limerick, were apparently present when the
troops marched into Rathkeale.[1] On 10 August it announced
that 'The two last strongholds of the Irregulars in County
Limerick – Abbeyfeale and Dromcolloger' – had been captured
the previous day.[2] The same edition included a story under the
screaming headline of 'Sacrilegious Outrage – Irregular Who
Went To Mass With Bombs':

At the early Mass in Rathkeale on Sunday last [5 August] – apparently because Canon O'Donnell, V.P., had been for weeks past, advising the people to abide by democratic government – an irregular went into the church with two bombs, avowing in very blasphemous language that he would 'do for' the Canon. Some friend of the irregular followed him into the church and succeeded in getting him to leave without perpetrating any outrage.[3]

O'Duffy himself reviewed the forward march of his troops in the South Western Command shortly after the fall of Kilmallock:

On the 1st August we held East and Mid Limerick from the Tipperary border to the river Maigue. We have since crossed the Maigue and captured Adare, Rathkeale and Newcastlewest, twelve miles beyond the river, clearing all small posts like Kilmacow, Kilfinny and Ballingarry on the way. The country being close and thickly wooded the utmost caution was preserved … our Troops had captured Newcastlewest … We have also captured a large number of prisoners. The irregulars have also been cleared from Askeaton, Foynes and Glin, and with the exception of concentrations, at Abbeyfeale on the Kerry border and Dromcollogher on the Cork border, they are now completely routed from County Limerick.

The Limerick City irregulars, with the remnants of their leaders, are now reported at Abbeyfeale. After the surrender of Limerick they fled to Patrickswell, thence to Adare, thence in rapid succession to Rathkeale, to Newcastle, to Abbeyfeale.

As was anticipated Kilmallock fell shortly after the capture of Bruree, and when the National Troops had established themselves on the East and West flanks. We now strongly hold a line three miles south of Kilmallock, adding Galbally to our list of posts on the left flank. On the East our advance has been even more marked. We have established a strong outpost at Newport, Co. Tipperary, and extended the line Pallas-Oola to Tipperary Town, taking control of Limerick Junction, a most important post.[4]

Clearly, then, the Bruff-Bruree-Kilmallock triangle was not the only zone where the war was going favourably for the National Army. The West Limerick Brigade had been primarily anti-Treaty and Brigadier Garret McAuliffe detailed the preparations he was making for the defence of West Limerick to his superiors in the 1st Southern Division some weeks before the pro-Treaty onslaught:

I have the following bridges in Adare–Croom destroyed …

(a) Railway Bridge at Adare (destroyed)

(b) River Bridge at Adare (destroyed)

(c) Ferry Bridge (destroyed)

(d) Two strong bridges over the Maigue, in Adare Manor Estate

(e) Work on Castle Roberts Bridge being carried out

O.C. Mid-Limerick has taken over Adare with 20 riflemen, in addition 30 riflemen are [in] Rathkeale as reserve.

McAuliffe was short of explosives and asked, 'Could you send

gelignite, tonite [*sic*] or guncotton?'[5] The Republicans, in an
effort to obstruct the pro-Treaty advance, were sabotaging the
bridges as they withdrew further into west Limerick. Most
of the bridges mentioned in this despatch by McAuliffe were
destroyed on Monday 24 July.[6] In an October 1923 report,
presumably to IRA GHQ, McAuliffe gave an overview of the
course of the Civil War in west Limerick:

> … we contested every foot of the area with the advancing
> enemy, who numbered 1,500 with artillery, armoured cars etc.
> We had but 100 men of the West Limerick Brigade including
> some men of the Mid Lim[eric]k Brigade. Although men were
> then idle in some areas in 1st Southern Division, we did not get
> assistance in these engagements from Div[ision]. In subsequent
> activities the following enemy posts were attacked and captured:
>
> Foynes (twice)
>
> Abbeyfeale
>
> Rathkeale
>
> Tarbert
>
> In addition there were other engagements with the enemy,
> besides the usual activities in connection with Railways, P.O.s,
> etc. as laid down in General Orders.
>
> Over 100 rifles were captured from the enemy.
>
> Owing to an unfortunate strike [*sic*] of ill-luck the Brigade
> staff were captured by enemy early in the war and I myself had
> to undergo a very serious surgical operation with the result
> that I was unfit for active service for a period of four months.
>
> Owing to the scarcity of ammunition almost all those rifles
> had to be dumped.[7]

McAuliffe also reflected on his Civil War experience in conversation with Ernie O'Malley:

> Foynes I captured. I got no orders ... I captured the place in thirty minutes and I got thirty rifles ... We captured Abbeyfeale when we got 30 to 40 rifles. We surprised them there. Michael Colivet attacked Rathkeale and he might have taken it only reinforcements came on. Then Mick Colivet recaptured Foynes when he got thirty to forty rifles.[8]

As the attack on Kilmallock began on Friday morning, 4 August, it was paralleled by a simultaneous thrust from Patrickswell towards Adare and further westwards, which made significant progress. Having recaptured Patrickswell on 3 August, National Army forces under Brigadier Michael Keane, Colonel Tom Keogh and Colonel Jimmy Slattery seized Adare at 7 p.m. on 4 August, but only after overcoming determined resistance. The troops had marched from Patrickswell in the early hours of Friday and it was 'a dripping but not dispirited crew', according to an *Irish Times* correspondent, who approached the outskirts of Adare at 4 a.m.[9] Having expended considerable energy in clearing felled trees from the road, the troops also found themselves short of rations. They made contact with the IRA outposts at 5 a.m. The attackers had converged on the village from two points but were pinned down at the far side of the Maigue by heavy machine-gun and rifle fire, the bridge having been sabotaged:

> Both spans had been cut across in a way which made the

passage of any wheeled vehicle, gun or armoured car, impossible, the gaps being over seven feet wide. Infantry, by walking along the parapets, or jumping the opening, could just get across.[10]

The Republican fire was directed mainly from a church which lay about 100 yards back from the opposite bank of the river, so a crossing by infantry unsupported by artillery was not a realistic option for the Free State. The artillery was on the way, however. A suitable firing position for the eighteen-pound gun was located on a path along a narrow lane a few hundred yards back from the bridge. The gun was dragged into position by a Whippet. The *Irish Times* correspondent's description of how it was put into action must have delighted the Free State censor:

> The gunners crouched behind the shields, and then it was discovered, when the trail had been secured, that a fence-post was in the way. One of the gunners seized an axe and went forward. A bullet hit the head of the axe. The gunner went forward. A bullet splintered the handle. The gunner went forward. A bullet tore his tunic. The gunner went forward. Two swift blows, a wrench of the stake, and the field of fire was free. Then the gunner went backward, and the gun took up his side of the argument.[11]

The first two shells hit the church where the IRA machine gunners were perched in the tower. The Dunraven Arms Hotel, where the Republicans had set up their HQ, was also hit. The publicity department of the South Western Command announced that when the troops entered the hotel 'all the rooms in the building were found to be bespattered with blood, showing that there must have been fairly severe casualties amongst the irregulars'.[12]

Michael Hartney, one of the IRA leaders, was badly wounded there. Hartney's wife, Mary, according to an IRA list of Mid Limerick Brigade casualties, was 'Killed in Adare while attending our troops.'[13] She was hit by shellfire while working in the first aid centre at the Dunraven Arms and was one of only a few members of Cumann na mBan killed in either the War of Independence or the Civil War. She was buried in Mount St Lawrence Cemetery on Monday 7 August, her body having been brought back to the city by a circuitous route from Newcastlewest the previous night. The *Limerick Chronicle* maintained a dignified and respectful tone when reporting on funerals and recorded that 'the cortege was of large and representative portions, and expressed the sympathy felt for the husband and family of the deceased'.[14]

Apart from the Dunraven Arms and the church, the buildings around Adare went largely untouched. There is no truth in the rumour in circulation around Limerick at the time that Adare Manor, the residence of the Earl of Dunraven, was burned by Republicans. National troops occupied the manor.

Rathkeale was also taken on 4 August despite the desertion of some of the Curragh Reserve men.[15] The limited fighting that took place in Rathkeale was directed towards impeding pro-Treaty efforts to position the eighteen-pounder. The Republicans in the old RIC barracks in Rathkeale capitulated almost as soon as the first artillery shells were fired, however. Askeaton was already in Free State hands so they headed for Newcastlewest. As they passed through Ardagh they resembled 'a weary bedraggled lot, trudging along in disparate groups, with seemingly very little fight left in them'. However, they marched into Newcastlewest 'in orderly ranks, four deep and in step ... about two hundred of them'.[16]

Newcastlewest was something of an exception in west Limerick, in that most of the IRA members there went pro-Treaty. The pro-Treatyites were quartered at Castleview, while the anti-Treaty section retained the buildings originally taken over from the British – the local RIC barracks and Devon Castle. McAuliffe established his HQ at Devon Castle. When the Civil War commenced the Castleview garrison went to Limerick city to assist the Free State forces there.[17] The *Limerick Chronicle* of 8 August carried a detailed and sometimes imaginative account of the Free State advance from Rathkeale to Newcastlewest, the twelve-hour confrontation involving pro-Treaty artillery and armoury, and the Republican evacuation that ensued after the burning of Devon Castle:

> The troops moved from Rathkeale at three o'clock this morning, and a determined assault was made half an hour later. The fight lasted till nearly 3 o'clock this afternoon, when an advance party of troops entered the town. They were given a wonderful reception. The military operations were conducted by Brigadier Slattery, of the Dublin Guards, and three high explosive shells were used in the attack. Under cover of darkness the troops pressed forward from Rathkeale. The morning was bitterly cold but the advance was continued, despite the

numerous barricades which blocked the roads leading to Newcastlewest. Little opposition was encountered until the National Army had penetrated the irregular lines to within a quarter of a mile of the town. There were, however, several sharp skirmishes on the way, and in all of these the unseen irregular sharpshooters suffered reverses. The flash and report of a gun were the only means the troops had of locating the attackers, but so accurate and deadly was their return fire that the irregulars made off helter-skelter towards the town.

Approaching Newcastlewest the infantry split up, one section taking a circuitous route, while the remainder, with the transport, pushed on through Ardagh. The entire detachment was a relatively small one. In the early stages of the fighting five irregulars were taken prisoners. When a point was reached some few hundred yards away from the town a veritable debacle set in among the irregulars who fled in disorder from their positions, which were of a formidable nature. The troops rushed an armoured car into the market place and a spray of machine gun fire poured on the irregulars, who thereby suffered heavy casualties. Ten were killed outright. This success was pressed home by a salvo of artillery fire directed at the outskirts of the irregular headquarters, Devon Castle. So far had the troops pierced the lines that it was possible to carry out the shelling operations from the castle demesne. The thunder of the big guns proved too much for the occupants, who flocked out of the building and beat a hasty retreat along the Cork road. Before they left, it is stated that the castle was set on fire. A stately eighteenth-century structure, it has suffered serious damage, and is almost a total ruin.

The most glaring inaccuracy in this report relates to the casualty figures quoted. Only two IRA Volunteers were killed during the attack. These were the two O'Dwyer brothers from Limerick city, Cornelius and Edward, who were killed fighting for the IRA in Newcastlewest on 7 August.[18] One was killed in a quarry at Churchtown. The other was killed two hours later in an engagement in a field adjacent to the Cork road. It was from this direction that the flank of the attack, under Keane, entered the town, having moved along the Bruff Line. The Dublin Guard, under Keogh and Slattery, had taken the main road from Rathkeale and entered Newcastlewest under the cover of an armoured car.

The Cork Republican units had retreated to Buttevant before the attack started and left the defence of the town to 150 West Limerick Brigade Republicans, fifty Mid Limerick Brigade men and a small section of Kerry No. 1 Brigade Volunteers. Keogh's by now tried and trusted policy of sending skirmishing parties of the Dublin Guard ahead of the main body of troops to establish a firing site for the artillery, was again implemented, but it was 3 p.m. by the time the eighteen-pounder was brought to bear on the anti-Treaty positions, which suggests that the Republican defence of Newcastlewest was tenacious. This is not surprising, given the calibre of men like Michael Colbert, Owen McAuliffe, Con Cregan, Tadhg Crowley, Jimmy Crowley and James Collins, as well as Garret McAuliffe, all of them War of Independence veterans. As in Adare and Rathkeale only a few shells were fired, in this case three or perhaps four, but their effect was devastating. The two shells which hit Devon Castle may have started the fire or it may have been set alight deliberately by its defenders.[19]

CONCLUSION

With the Limerick–Waterford line smashed and the advance into north Kerry going well, the National Army was able to turn to Cork. By 13 August they had taken both Charleville and Buttevant without a fight. The sea landings in Cork had also been successful and Republicans abandoned the city on 10/11 August and evacuated towns around the county. The anti-Treaty IRA decided to revert to guerrilla warfare and the conventional phase of the Civil War was over. The battle for Kilmallock had been the last of the large-scale, deliberately planned, field actions.

Republicans may have lost the urban centres but there were still large swathes of countryside without any Free State presence. The National Army acknowledged that the anti-Treatyites had not been defeated and continued to pose a threat:

> The Irregulars in Cork and Kerry are still more or less intact. Our forces have captured towns, but they have not captured Irregulars and arms on anything like a large scale, and, until this is done, the Irregulars will be capable of guerrilla warfare.[1]

Even if they had not been defeated, many Republicans were demoralised and withdrew from the fray at this stage.[2] Nevertheless, the war dragged on until the following April/May as the most committed anti-Treatyites continued to defend the Republic.

The IRA had been on the back foot for most of the war and were shadow-boxing, while the National Army, having circled its opponent long enough to be satisfied with its own condition, adopted the more aggressive stance. Once the war started, it may have been too late for the anti-Treatyites to regain the initiative, but they made little enough effort to do so at any point. In the early conventional stages of the conflict, the use of artillery gave the pro-Treaty forces a clear advantage wherever Republicans tried to make a stand in fixed positions, including Dublin, Waterford, Limerick, Kilmallock, Adare, Rathkeale and Newcastlewest. The IRA had fought hard in some of these places, but not in others.

The battle for Kilmallock involved a curious mix of resolute defence, desperate counter-attack, and finally precipitous and abrupt retreat. It was not that the Republicans were unwilling to engage the Free Staters, for they had done so for almost two weeks in the Bruff-Bruree-Kilmallock triangle. They had shown their mettle and their fighting qualities in these exchanges.

The reasons the Republicans chose to evacuate Kilmallock are clear: the National Army had successfully opened up a second front in the rear of the Munster Republic, landing troops at strategically significant locations on the south and south-west coasts, and exposing the defenders of Kilmallock to the dangers of being outflanked and surrounded. The coastal attacks had also played on the local loyalties of the Kerry and Cork contingents at Kilmallock.

Despite these considerations and the reasonable response to them, the feeling persists that the early retreat represented something of a missed opportunity for the Republicans.

Kilmallock, as long as the surrounding hills were held, was an eminently defendable strong point: one of the last that the Republicans still occupied in early August. The defenders, both officers and rank and file, were experienced and battle-hardened. They were well-enough equipped to significantly deplete and debilitate the pro Treaty forces, and to disrupt and delay their advance to the south and south-west. The fall of Kilmallock was a major part of the disintegration of the Munster Republic. The availability of artillery to the National Army and the inability of the IRA to react to that threat or to neutralise it was once again a crucial factor.

A critical evaluation of Republican decision-making at this point is necessary to form a sense of what the battle for Kilmallock indicates about the Civil War in a wider context. In general terms, there are question marks over the effective functioning of the anti-Treaty chain of command and communications, and the relationship between central and local sources of authority. Systems failures often resulted in a lack of coordination between IRA units, but the same charge can be levelled against the National Army.

Liam Deasy's command at Kilmallock had been beset by problems. Some of the discord between the anti-Treatyites had spilled over from Limerick city because Liam Lynch's failure to press home his early advantages there had led to frustration and dissension. The simmering discontent within Republican ranks was directed mainly against the senior command and was not without justification.

Lynch was in a dominant position in Limerick but because

of his hesitancy to fight old comrades he refused to attack weak pro-Treaty positions and gave Michael Brennan invaluable time and space in which to strengthen his hand. Internal rivalries between Cork and Limerick IRA columns in Kilmallock exacerbated rather than alleviated existing tensions. If Deasy did not have full control over his forces, this would have reduced the confidence, coherence and unity of the Republican leadership. Eoin O'Duffy and W. R. E. Murphy, on the other hand, compensated for the shortcomings of their troops by presenting a unified and well-coordinated command structure.

It is not clear if the decision of the Cork and Kerry IRA units to withdraw from Kilmallock was made on their own account or in consultation with Deasy, but it had serious repercussions for the Republicans. Within two weeks of the fall of Kilmallock, the National Army had assumed total and unchallenged mastery of every significant population centre in the north of Munster as Republican resistance in the region evaporated. This could only have had a demoralising effect on Republicans and an invigorating effect on Free Staters.

The apparent imminence of Free State victory was partly due to a change in Republican tactics based on the recognition that the defence of towns like Kilmallock was no longer a realistic option. Lynch had been mulling over a return to all-out guerrilla tactics as early as 25 July, although he did not as yet consider them necessary or even desirable around Kilmallock. In light of events in the previous days, he was confident of success in what he termed 'open country' in east Limerick and believed that the IRA should maintain fixed positions in the area.[3]

On 9 August Lynch had informed Ernie O'Malley that

'Owing to developments in Cork … our forces on this front [around Kilmallock] have been reduced, and are forming into columns.'[4] Orders issued by Deasy on 12 August confirm the policy of retreat and explain the rationale behind it:

> As a result of the enemy invading the divisional area in numbers much larger than our available armed forces, verbal instructions to vacate all barracks and form into columns are hereby confirmed. Only the very best and most experienced men. Maximum strength of the column thirty-five men.[5]

One week later, on 19 August, Lynch confirmed Deasy's orders: 'Our troops will now be formed into ASUs [active service units] and operate in the open.'[6] The IRA had officially returned to guerrilla warfare and the reference to 'verbal instructions' points to the possibility of fundamental and wide-ranging communication and command problems within Republican ranks. It creates the impression of decisions of paramount strategic importance being taken in an ad hoc and piecemeal fashion, and that Deasy and Lynch, as senior officers, had been usurped or pre-empted by local junior officers. However, reliance on verbal communication was simply the reality of the situation for Republican forces at this stage, but the instructions being delivered had been prepared, in some version at least, over several weeks.

The post-Kilmallock headlong retreat, then, may not have been the result of sudden and contagious panic after all, but a pre-planned reaction that seems logical, feasible and justifiable in light of the dire circumstances in which the Republican forces found themselves after Kilmallock. It may not have immediately alleviated any of the pressure under which the IRA was straining, but it guaranteed the medium-term survival of the anti-Treaty movement in an impossible situation.

After the battle for Kilmallock the scales of military advantage were tipped almost completely in favour of the National Army. The war began to degenerate into a pattern of vindictive reprisals and tit-for-tat killings. This phase, brutal and bitter, was marked by a cycle of atrocities in areas where the anti-Treaty guerrilla campaign was most tenacious. The Public Safety Bill of September, which came a month after the death from illness of Arthur Griffith and the death-in-action of Michael Collins, signified that the Free State was about to institute martial law. The government, relying heavily on its capacity for violence to assert its authority, embarked on a concerted policy of executing Republican prisoners. There were at least seventy-seven such official executions under a variety of emergency powers legislation and many more non-judicial executions. Republicans engaged in a campaign of assassinations. The most notorious of the atrocities were probably those in Kerry in March 1923. Five National Army soldiers were killed by a mine at Knocknagoshel on 6 March. In the following weeks, seventeen IRA prisoners were killed by mines, a number of others were summarily shot dead in equally murky circumstances, and five were officially executed. The Dublin Guard was heavily involved. As the situation degenerated in Kerry, Dublin and Cork, Limerick was less volatile, with relatively few deaths in combat or killings in cold blood after August 1922. There were a number of related reasons for this: the departure of the Cork and Kerry IRA units, which had done much of the fighting in the city and county: the over-whelmingly strong National Army presence; and the gravitation of Limerick anti-Treatyites to more fertile ground elsewhere. But the war was by no means a tame affair in Limerick. Four anti-Treatyites were killed while prisoners and there were two judicial executions. One unarmed, off-duty National Army soldier was assassinated, and another died after being beaten by his IRA captors.[7]

The battle for Limerick city had claimed the lives of as many civilians as it did combatants (six pro-Treaty and five anti-Treaty) due to the high population density in the city and the concentrated nature of the fighting there. The level of casualties during the battle for Kilmallock, even though it was also one of the most important battles of the Civil War and lasted longer than the battle for Limerick city, and despite the multiple fa-talities at Ballingaddy and Ballygibba Cross, was much lower. Seven Free State soldiers were killed in those incidents. William Dunworth, killed at Bruff, was the only non-affiliated civilian killed. Mary Hartney, killed at Adare, may not have been a combatant but she was a member of Cumann na mBan, a con-stituent part of the anti-Treaty Republican movement. There were at least three IRA men killed, namely Henry Meaney at Patrickswell and the O'Dwyer brothers at Newcastlewest.[8] This represents a minimum of twelve fatalities overall.

It seems that there may have been several other IRA Volunteers killed, however. Pádraig Óg Ó Ruairc referred to a Volunteer Slattery killed at Crossagalla during the Republican retreat from Limerick city. Connie Neenan recalled the death of a Volunteer Spillane at Broadford and Padraic O'Farrell's

Who's Who in the Irish War of Independence and Civil War lists a Maurice Spillane as being killed in action at Broadford in June 1922. Tom Doyle noted that Charles Hanlon of Listowel was wounded in Bruree on 26 July and died of his wounds on 4 August. O'Farrell, however, put Hanlon's death after the ceasefire of May 1923. Mainchín Seoighe suggested that when a Republican position near Quarry Hill came under fire on 28 July, Donal Murphy of Tulladuff, Liscarroll, north Cork, was killed.[8] This would make a total of sixteen fatalities.

There are a number of reasons why casualty figures are so difficult to determine. Both sides seemed loath to issue their own official casualty lists. Reports on enemy casualties from official sources were grossly exaggerated as routine. There wee issues of propaganda and morale at stake here, especially in the light of casualty rates that were relatively low. There was also a need to justify fighting a civil war that involved thousands of troops, the shelling by the Provisional Government of Irish towns and cities, and incidents such as the destruction of the Public Records Office at the Four Courts. Perhaps such actions could appear to be partly legitimised by claiming to have killed significant numbers of the enemy.

The subject of fatalities was often treated with a certain vagueness that sometimes bordered on contempt, particularly by the Provisional Government. While those who died fighting for Ireland in 1916 or during the War of Independence duly assumed their place in the pantheon of martyrs, those who died in the uniform of the National Army during the Civil War were disposable and were not always even afforded the dignity of having their death properly recorded. This is an indictment of the Free State. Political posturing aside, Republicans at least honoured their dead in a more suitable fashion.

Karl Murphy, in his study of his grandfather W. R. E. Murphy, recounts an apocryphal tale 'which could only have taken place on an Irish battlefield with Irish soldiers involved' and which apparently occurred during the battle for Kilmallock: 'the Angelus Bell sounded out … Still under fire the men sank to their knees amidst the bullets to say their prayers.'[9] This story may or may not contain an element of truth. Many battlefield situations are likely to involve individuals who would indeed prefer to pray rather than to shoot. However, the notion that part of the reason Civil War casualties were so low was an absence of the will to kill is little more than a comforting myth. When the shelling and shooting started, it displaced the initial general hesitancy to fight. A growing resentment and ruthlessness, that eventually manifested in reprisal atrocities, was clearly evident during the battle for Kilmallock.

Endnotes

Introduction

1   Liam Deasy, *Brother against Brother* (Cork, 1998), p. 66.

2   Joe Lee, 'The Background: Anglo-Irish relations, 1898–1921', in Cormac O'Malley and Anne Dolan (eds), *'No Surrender Here!': The Civil War Papers of Ernie O'Malley* (Dublin, 2007).

3   'East Limerick' refers to an IRA brigade, or the territory encompassed by that brigade, or to an electoral constituency, whereas 'east Limerick' is simply a geographical area.

4   Liam Manahan (University College Dublin Archives [UCDA], Ernie O'Malley Notebooks [EOMN], P17b/117, p. 35).

5   *Limerick Leader*, 2 January 1922.

6   Brian Murphy, 'The Civil War 1922–23: An anti-Treaty perspective', *The Irish Sword – The Civil War, 1922–23*, vol. xx, no. 82 (winter 1997), p. 298.

7   UCDA, Desmond Fitzgerald Papers, P80/312.

8   Quoted in Mainchín Seoighe, *The Story of Kilmallock* (Kilmallock, 1987), p. 290.

9   John Pinkman [Francis E. Maguire (ed.)], *In the Legion of the Vanguard* (Cork, 1998), p. 148.

10   *Ibid.*, p. 152.

11   Murphy, 'The Civil War 1922–23', p. 297.

12   Pádraig Óg Ó Ruairc, *The Battle for Limerick city* (Cork, 2010).

13   Quoted in Michael Hopkinson, *Green against Green: The Irish Civil War* (Dublin, 2004), p. 146.

14   Karl Murphy, 'General W.R.E. Murphy and the Irish Civil War' (MA Thesis, National University of Ireland, Maynooth, 1994).

15   Ó Ruairc, *The Battle for Limerick city*, pp. 43, 54, 66.

16   Murphy, 'General W.R.E. Murphy', pp. 5–7.

17   Hopkinson, *Green against Green*, p. 151.

18   Calton Younger, *Ireland's Civil War* (London, 1968), pp. 396–7.

19   Ó Ruairc, *The Battle for Limerick city*, p. 138.

20   Hopkinson, *Green against Green*, pp. 272–3.

21   Pinkman, *In the Legion of the Vanguard*, p. 148.

22   Eoin Neeson, *The Civil War in Ireland* (Cork, 1966).

23   Michael Hopkinson, 'The Civil War from the pro-Treaty perspective', *The Irish Sword – The Civil War, 1922–23*, vol. xx, no. 82 (winter 1997), p. 289.

24   John Regan, *The Irish Counter-Revolution, 1921–36* (Dublin, 1999), p. 80.

25   Hopkinson, *Green against Green*, p. 290.

26   Pinkman, *In the Legion of the Vanguard*, p. 155.

27   *Limerick Chronicle*, 1 August 1922.

Chapter 1

1   Strickland, HQ British Army 6th Division, Cork, to GHQ British Army Ireland, 22 August 1921 (Imperial War Museum, Strickland Papers).

2   Hopkinson, *Green against Green*, p. 15.

3   'Breaches of the Truce' (National Archives United Kingdom [NAUK], Colonial Office [CO] 904/154).

4   UCDA, Richard Mulcahy Papers [RMP], P7A/23; UCDA, EOMP, P17a/9.

5   GHQ to 2nd Southern Division (UCDA, Con Moloney Papers [CMP], P9/196).

6   Daily summaries, 19 November 1921 (NAUK, CO 904/147).

7   Daily summaries, 23 November 1921 (NAUK, CO 904/147).

8   *Limerick Leader*, 16 December 1921.

9   Maurice Meade (National Archives of Ireland, Bureau of Military History Witness Statement 891, pp. 43–4); Tomás Malone

(National Archives of Ireland, Bureau of Military History Witness Statement 845, p. 94); Tomás Malone (UCDA, EOMN, P17b/106, pp. 94–5).

10   UCDA, RMP, P7B/71.

11   Garret McAuliffe (UCDA, EOMN, P17b/124).

12   Adjutant Subdivisional Area to Adjutant 1st Southern Division, 17 October 1922 (UCDA, EOMP, P17a/88).

13   UCDA, EOMP, P17a/88.

14   Seoighe, *The Story of Kilmallock*, pp. 287–9.

Chapter 2

1   Mossie Harnett [James Joy (ed.)], *Victory and Woe: The West Limerick Brigade in the War of Independence* (Dublin, 2002), pp. 130, 135.

2   Uinseann MacEoin, *Survivors* (Dublin, 1980), pp. 244–6.

3   *Sgéal Chatha Luimnighe*, 11 August 1922.

4   MacEoin, *Survivors*, pp. 230–2.

5   Hopkinson, *Green against Green*, p. 150.

6   Con Moloney to Ernie O'Malley, Old Barracks, Fermoy, 25 July 1922 (UCDA, Moss Twomey Papers [MTP], P69/77).

7   Murphy, 'General W.R.E. Murphy', pp. 5–7.

8   Fearghal McGarry, *Eoin O'Duffy: Self-Made Hero* (Oxford, 2005), p. 109.

9   Con Moloney to Ernie O'Malley, Old Barracks, Fermoy, 18 July 1922 (UCDA, EOMP, P171/60).

10   *Ibid.*

11   Hopkinson, *Green against Green*, pp. 153–5.

12   Younger, *Ireland's Civil War*, p. 393.

13   Hopkinson, *Green against Green*, pp. 151–2.

14   Quoted in Michael Harrington, *The Munster Republic: The Civil War in North Cork* (Cork, 2009), p. 57.

15   *Sgéal Chatha Luimnighe*, 28 July 1922.

16 Frank O'Connor, *An Only Child* (Dublin, 1969), pp. 215–6.

17 Hopkinson, *Green against Green*, pp. 150–1.

18 O'Connor, *An Only Child*, pp. 216–7.

19 Con Moloney to Ernie O'Malley, Old Barracks, Fermoy, 18 July 1922 (UCDA, EOMP, P17a/60).

20 Hopkinson, *Green against Green*, p. 151.

21 *Ibid.*, p. 152.

22 *Ibid.*

23 Murphy, 'General W.R.E. Murphy', p. 8.

24 Paul Walsh, 'The Irish Civil War, 1922–23: A military study of the conventional phase, 28 June–11 August 1922' (New York Military Affairs Symposium, City University of New York Graduate Centre, 11 December 1998).

25 UCDA, RMP, P7/B/68.

26 *Limerick Chronicle*, 29 July 1922; *Sgéal Chatha Luimnighe*, 31 July 1922.

27 Deasy, *Brother against Brother*, p. 66.

28 Hopkinson, *Green against Green*, p. 150.

29 Con Moloney to Ernie O'Malley, 13 July 1922 (UCDA, EOMP, P17a/60); UCDA, MTP, P69/77 (105-5); Ó Ruairc, *The Battle for Limerick city*, p. 88; Deasy, *Brother against Brother*, p. 71.

30 *Sgéal Chatha Luimnighe*, 11 August 1922; *Limerick Chronicle*, 12 August 1922.

31 *The Cork Examiner*, 16 July 1922; *Limerick Chronicle*, 25 July 1922.

32 *The Freeman's Journal*, 24 July 1922.

33 *Republican Bulletin*, 19 July 1922.

34 UCDA, RMP, P7/B/21.

35 Con Moloney to Ernie O'Malley, Old Barracks, Fermoy, 18 July 1922 (UCDA, EOMP, P171a/60).

36 Hopkinson, *Green against Green*, p. 152.

37 MacEoin, *Survivors*, p. 231.

38 *Limerick Chronicle*, 25 July 1922.

39 Quoted in Harrington, *The Munster Republic*, p. 61.

40   MacEoin, *Survivors*, pp. 231–2.

41   Albert Ross, 'The siege of Bruff 1922', *Lough Gur Historical Society Journal*, 5 (1989), pp. 14–5.

42   *The Freeman's Journal*, 25 July 1922.

43   *Limerick Chronicle*, 25 July 1922.

44   *Ibid.*, 11–22 July 1922; Ross, 'The siege of Bruff', p. 15.

45   Con Moloney to Ernie O'Malley, Old Barracks, Fermoy, 25 July 1922 (UCDA MTP, P69/77).

46   Ó Ruairc, *The Battle for Limerick city*, p. 125.

47   *Ibid.*, p. 128.

48   Con Moloney to Ernie O'Malley, Old Barracks, Fermoy, 25 July 1922 (UCDS, EOMP, P69/77).

49   Liam Lynch to Ernie O'Malley, Field General Headquarters, IRA Barracks, Fermoy, 25 July 1922 (UCDA, EOMP, P17a/60).

50   Harrington, *The Munster Republic*, p. 60.

51   Hopkinson, *Green against Green*, p. 151.

52   *Sgéal Chatha Luimnighe*, 25 July 1922; *Limerick Chronicle*, 25 July 1922 (quote found in both).

53   Neeson, *The Civil War in Ireland*, p. 134.

54   O'Connor, *An Only Child*, p. 227.

55   *The Cork Examiner*, 26 July 1922.

56   Neeson, *The Civil War*, p. 135; Younger, *Ireland's Civil War*, p. 394; Seoighe, *The Story of Kilmallock*, p. 291; South-Western Command daily report, 4th Southern Division, Rockbarton, to GHQ, 4 August 1922 (UCDA, RMP, P7/B/39).

57   South-Western Command daily report, 4th Southern Division, Rockbarton, to GHQ, 4 August 1922 (UCDA, RMP, P7/B/39).

58   Neeson, *The Civil War*, p. 135.

59   *Limerick Chronicle*, 29 July 1922.

60   Field GHQ, Kerry Command, Tralee, 13 February 1924 (Irish Military Archives, Military Service Pension Collection, 2D152 [Cornelius Sullivan]).

61   Liam Lynch to Ernie O'Malley, Field General Headquarters, IRA

Barracks, Fermoy, 25 July 1922 (UCDA, EOMP, P17a/60).

62 Con Moloney to Ernie O'Malley, Field General Headquarters, IRA Barracks, Fermoy, 29 July 1922 (UCDA, EOMP, P17a/60).

63 UCDA, EOMP, P17a/60.

Chapter 3

1 Seoighe, *The Story of Kilmallock*, pp. 291–2.

2 Quoted in Harrington, *The Munster Republic,* p. 62.

3 *Sgéal Chatha Luimnighe*, 28 July 1922.

4 *Limerick Chronicle*, 29 July 1922.

5 Harrington, *The Munster Republic*, p. 62.

6 Pinkman, *In the Legion of the Vanguard*, pp. 155–6.

7 *The Cork Examiner*, 31 July 1922.

8 Murphy, 'General W.R.E. Murphy', p. 9.

9 Neeson, *The Civil War*, p. 136.

10 *Limerick Chronicle*, 3 August 1922; *Sgéal Chatha Luimnighe*, 3 August 1922; *The Freeman's Journal*, 3 August 1922.

11 Harrington, *The Munster Republic,* p. 63.

12 Deasy, *Brother against Brother*, p. 71.

13 Neeson, *The Civil War*, p. 107.

14 *Limerick Chronicle*, 7 September 1968.

15 *Limerick Chronicle*, 3 August 1922.

16 *Ibid.*; *Sgéal Chatha Luimnighe*, 3 August 1922.

17 *Limerick Chronicle*, 5 August 1922.

18 *Limerick Leader*, 13 August 1983 (the article was originally written in 1933).

19 Pinkman, *In the Legion of the Vanguard*, pp. 157–60.

20 South Western Command daily report, 4th Southern Division, Rockbarton, to GHQ, 3 August 1922 (UCDA, RMP, P7/B/68); *Sgéal Chatha Luimnighe*, 4 August 1922; *Limerick Chronicle*, 3 August 1922; Harrington, *The Munster Republic*, pp. 63–4; Neeson, *The Civil War*, pp. 136–8; Younger, *Ireland's Civil War*, p. 395.

21 Walsh, 'The Irish Civil War'.

22   Murphy, 'General W.R.E. Murphy', pp. 15–16.

Chapter 4

1   *Sgéal Chatha Luimnighe*, 28 and 31 July 1922.

2   Murphy, 'General W.R.E. Murphy', pp. 11–12.

3   UCDA, RMP, P7/B/68.

4   *Ibid.*

5   Murphy, 'General W.R.E. Murphy', p. 12.

6   UCDA, RMP, P7B/68.

7   Hopkinson, *Green against Green*, p. 152.

8   Tom Doyle, *The Summer Campaign in Kerry* (Cork, 2010), p. 55.

9   UCDA, RMP, P7B/68.

10   *The New York Times*, 5 August 1922.

11   Neeson, *The Civil War*, p. 139.

12   UCDA, RMP, P7B/68.

13   *The New York Times*, 5 August 1922.

14   UCDA, RMP, P7B/68.

15   *The New York Times*, 5 August 1922.

16   *The Freeman's Journal*, 7 August 1922.

17   UCDA, RMP, P7B/68.

18   *The New York Times*, 6 August 1922.

19   *Sgéal Chatha Luimnighe*, 8 August 1922; *Limerick Chronicle*, 8 August 1922.

20   *Limerick Chronicle*, 5 August 1922.

21   Seoighe, *The Story of Kilmallock*, p. 293.

22   *Limerick Chronicle*, 27 July 1922.

23   *Ibid.*, 8 August 1922.

24   Joseph M. Curran, *The Birth of the Irish Free State* (Alabama, 1980), p. 243.

25   Younger, *Ireland's Civil War*, pp. 396–7.

26   Harrington, *The Munster Republic*, p. 69.

27   Younger, *Ireland's Civil War*, pp. 396–7.

28 Doyle, *The Summer Campaign in Kerry*, p. 39.

29 Neeson, *The Civil War*, p. 140.

30 Doyle, *The Summer Campaign in Kerry*, p. 38.

31 Hopkinson, *Green against Green*, p. 137.

32 Walsh, 'The Irish Civil War'.

33 Neeson, *The Civil War*, p. 140.

34 Liam Lynch to Ernie O'Malley, Field General Headquarters, Fermoy, 9 August 1922 (UCDA, EOMP, P17a/60).

35 Hopkinson, *Green against Green*, pp. 163–6.

36 Deasy, *Brother against Brother*, p. 66.

Chapter 5

1 See also *Limerick Chronicle*, 8 August 1922.

2 See also *Limerick Chronicle*, 10 August 1922.

3 See also *Limerick Chronicle*, 8 August 1922.

4 *Sgéal Chatha Luimnighe*, 9 August 1922; *Limerick Chronicle*, 10 August 1922.

5 Garret McAuliffe, O/C West Limerick Brigade to 1st Southern Division, 24 July 1922 (UCDA, MPT, P69/24(108)).

6 *Limerick Chronicle*, 27 July 1922.

7 Report on West Limerick Brigade by Garret McAuliffe, O/C Brigade, 3 October 1923 (UCDA, EOMP, P69/114(19)).

8 Garret McAuliffe (UCDA, EOMN, P17b/124).

9 Quoted in the *Limerick Chronicle*, 8 August 1922.

10 *Ibid.*

11 *Ibid.*

12 *Limerick Chronicle*, 5 August 1922.

13 List of Mid Limerick Brigade casualties during the Civil War, May 1923 (UCDA, MTP, P69/114(22)).

14 *Limerick Chronicle*, 8 August 1922.

15 Hopkinson, *Green against Green*, pp. 152–3.

16 Michael Dore, 'The taking of Newcastlewest in the Civil War',

Newcastlewest Historical Journal (1987), pp. 8–9.

17   *Ibid.*, p. 7.

18   List of Mid Limerick Brigade casualties during the Civil War, May 1923 (UCDA, MTP, P69/114(22)).

19   Dore, 'The taking of Newcastlewest', pp. 10–11.

Conclusion

1   South Western Command report, 22 August 1922 (UCDA, RMP, P7/B/71).

2   Hopkinson, *Green against Green*, p. 165.

3   Liam Lynch to Ernie O'Malley, Field General Headquarters, IRA Barracks, Fermoy, 25 July 1922 (UCDA, EOMP, P17a/60).

4   Liam Lynch to Ernie O'Malley, Field General Headquarters, Fermoy, 9 August 1922 (UCDA, EOMP, P17a/60).

5   Quoted in Harrington, *The Munster Republic*, p. 77.

6   *Ibid.*

7   John O'Callaghan, *The Irish Revolution: Limerick, 1912–23* (Dublin, 2018), p. 111.

8   Ó Ruairc, *The Battle for Limerick city*, p. 128; Neenan quoted in MacEoin, *Survivors*, p. 244; Padraic O'Farrell, *Who's Who in the Irish War of Independence and Civil War, 1916–23* (Dublin, 1997), pp. 220–1; Doyle, *The Summer Campaign in Kerry*, p. 31; Seoighe, *The Story of Kilmallock*, p. 291.

9   Murphy, 'General W.R.E. Murphy', p. 12.

Bibliography

Archival Sources

Dublin

National Archives of Ireland (NAI):
>   Bureau of Military History Witness Statements

Irish Military Archives:
>   Military Service Pension Collection

University College Dublin Archives (UCDA):
>   Con Moloney Papers
>   Richard Mulcahy Papers
>   Ernie O'Malley Notebooks
>   Ernie O'Malley Papers
>   Moss Twomey Papers

London

Imperial War Museum:
>   General Sir Peter Strickland Papers

National Archives of the United Kingdom (NAUK):
>   Colonial Office Papers

Newspapers

Cork Examiner, The
Freeman's Journal, The
Limerick Chronicle
Limerick Leader

New York Times, The
Republican Bulletin
Sgéal Chatha Luimnighe

Books, Articles and Theses

Curran, Joseph M., *The Birth of the Irish Free State* (Alabama, 1980)

Deasy, Liam, *Brother against Brother* (Cork, 1998)

Dore, Michael, 'The taking of Newcastlewest in the Civil War', *Newcastlewest Historical Journal* (1987)

Doyle, Tom, *The Summer Campaign in Kerry* (Cork, 2010)

Harnett, Mossie [James Joy (ed.)], *Victory and Woe: The West Limerick Brigade in the War of Independence* (Dublin, 2002)

Harrington, Michael, *The Munster Republic: The Civil War in North Cork* (Cork, 2009)

Hopkinson, Michael, 'The Civil War from the pro-Treaty perspective', *The Irish Sword – The Civil War, 1922–23*, vol. xx, no. 82 (winter 1997), pp. 287–92

Hopkinson, Michael, *Green against Green: The Irish Civil War* (Dublin, 2004)

MacEoin, Uinseann, *Survivors* (Dublin, 1980)

McGarry, Fearghal, *Eoin O'Duffy: Self-Made Hero* (Oxford, 2005)

Murphy, Brian, 'The Civil War 1922–23: An anti-Treaty perspective', *The Irish Sword – The Civil War, 1922–23*, vol. xx, no. 82 (winter 1997), pp. 293–307

Murphy, Karl, 'General W.R.E. Murphy and the Irish Civil War' (MA Thesis, National University of Ireland, Maynooth, 1994)

Neeson, Eoin, *The Civil War in Ireland* (Cork, 1966)

O'Callaghan, John, *Revolutionary Limerick: The Republican Campaign for Independence in Limerick, 1913–21* (Dublin, 2010)

—— *The Irish Revolution: Limerick, 1912–23* (Dublin, 2018)

O'Connor, Frank, *An Only Child* (Dublin, 1969)

O'Farrell, Padraic, *Who's Who in the Irish War of Independence and Civil War, 1916–23* (Dublin, 1997)

O'Malley, Cormac, and Dolan, Anne (eds), *'No Surrender Here!': The Civil War Papers of Ernie O'Malley* (Dublin, 2007)

Ó Ruairc, Pádraig Óg, *The Battle for Limerick city* (Cork, 2010)

Pinkman, John [Francis E. Maguire (ed.)], *In the Legion of the Vanguard* (Cork, 1998)

Regan, John, *The Irish Counter-Revolution, 1921–36* (Dublin, 1999)

Ross, Albert, 'The siege of Bruff 1922', *Lough Gur Historical Society Journal*, 5 (1989)

Seoighe, Mainchín, *The Story of Kilmallock* (Kilmallock, 1987)

Walsh, Paul, 'The Irish Civil War, 1922–23: A military study of the conventional phase, 28 June–11 August 1922' (New York Military Affairs Symposium, City University of New York Graduate Centre, 11 December 1998)

Younger, Calton, *Ireland's Civil War* (London, 1968)

INDEX